HUNGRY HEART

Our three basic needs, for food and security and love, are so mixed and mingled and entwined that we cannot straightly think of one without the others. So it happens that when I write of hunger, I am really writing about love
M.F.K. Fisher

For Mum – my first feeder, and my first reader

HUNGRY HEART

A story of food and love

CLARE FINNEY

Aurum

Quarto

First published in 2023 by Aurum Press
an imprint of The Quarto Group.
One Triptych Place, London, SE1 9SH
United Kingdom
T (0)20 7700 6700
www.Quarto.com

A catalogue record for this book is available from the British Library.

ISBN 978-0-7112-6676-6
Ebook ISBN 978-0-7112-6678-0
Audiobook ISBN 978-0-7112-8597-2

10 9 8 7 6 5 4 3 2 1

Typeset in Garamond Premier Pro by SX Composing DTP,
Rayleigh, Essex, SS6 7EF

Printed by CPI Group (UK) Ltd, Croydon, CR0 4YY

Contents

PROLOGUE

I am four years old, standing on a three-legged stool in the middle of a clattering, steaming hotel kitchen. My grandmother – the hotel's proprietor – is stood behind me: one hand on my shoulder, the other guiding my own sticky hands which are clasped around a long wooden spoon. We're stirring flour, butter and sugar. The soft dust, sparkling crystals and canary yellow streaks of grease are level with my eyes, smearing the sides of the glass bowl as they meld together. To our right, a microwave pings; to our left, a 20-man toaster threatens to spring at any moment. My grandmother has guests to feed, rooms to clean and a family to tend to – but in that moment, with her hands around mine making millionaire's shortbread, we are together. I am immersed in love. I am immersed in food.

I am a food journalist. For seven years I have been talking, asking and writing about food for my living. Like you, I've also been eating it: with friends, family, partners, potential partners and on my own. I've cooked, been cooked for, eaten out, ordered in, and found that while my job dictates that the best meals are those made by the best chefs with the best ingredients, my life says food is only as good as the feelings that come with it. If I were to map out my life, it would more closely resemble a menu than it would a timeline or atlas: a compilation album of the dishes that define me by virtue of where I ate them and with whom.

That menu begins with shortbread in my grandparent's hotel kitchen: a playground of epic proportions, with spatulas and saucepan lids for swords and shields and a hotel-sized hotplate for a battleship. Indeed, this hotplate was where I spent much of my early years, its cosy confinement rendering it as apt for containing noisy, energetic grandchildren as for warming dishes. If my cousins were there we played, fuelled by the Crusha milkshakes our grandad whisked up in his magnificent frothing machine. There were kitchen utensils to 'row' with, balls of leftover pastry to shape, and – once we'd been set free – tubs of flour and semolina to stir, pat and dig in (environmental health officers weren't quite so rigorous back then). On my own, I read, or watched, mesmerised even then by the miracle that was my grandparents cooking and serving three courses to a 40-strong dining room.

Of course, the story of food and love long pre-dates my existence – even that of my grandparents. The inimitably human practice of forging relationships through food has been millennia in the making, and anthropologists have been chewing over how and why we do this for centuries. One of their most compelling theories is that our dining together was heralded by our being able to kill animals far larger than our individual appetites could stomach: in short, a slain mammoth was the primitive precursor to the neighbourhood hog roast. Add in fire and, later, agriculture and preservation techniques, and you have an approach to food that is almost entirely centred around communal living. At the same time, running quietly alongside this and cementing the connection in our minds, was our dopamine system which responds as powerfully to a loved one as it does a meal. Somewhere along the way, our brains began to associate these feasts with the people we ate them with. Love became bound up with breaking bread, sharing it and satiating our hunger for company as well as food.

The extraordinary significance of this development has been the lifelong specialist subject of Martin Jones, a professor of anthropology at Cambridge University. In his seminal book *Feast: Why Humans Share Food*, he observed that to any other species our practice of eating together – exposing our teeth, making direct eye contact, sharing food – would seem risky; but 'at some point our own ancestors turned those danger signals around and transformed them into the very essence of conviviality that defines humanity'. Once just/merely necessary fuel, to fight for and over, food became a medium of communication and social bonding, he continues. 'We now use the shared meal to punctuate the day, celebrate the great occasions of life, make transactions and define who is inside and outside any particular cultural group.'

This profound connection between food and love was with me in my grandma's hotel kitchen. It was with me every morning when my brother Nicholas and I snuck into our parents' bed for hot chocolate. It was with us post our parents' divorce, when food became a vital means of smoothing over the cracks and forging new families out of step-parents and step-siblings; and it undid me in Pizza Express when, aged sixteen and beset with eating disorders, I had a hotly anticipated date with Charlie, captain of the boy's school rugby team and popularly considered by the girls to be 'a solid eight out of ten'. 'I'll have chicken Caesar salad, please,' I whispered. 'Without the, um, chicken. Or dough sticks.' Charlie looked at me, perplexed. 'Is that a thing?' he asked, ordering himself cheesy garlic bread, pizza and dough balls. I don't know that my comprehensive rejection of sustenance was the reason I didn't secure a second date, but I do know, now, that one cannot love someone who doesn't love themselves – and that there is scant self-love in someone who denies themselves warm shredded chicken and batons of buttery dough.

This tortured relationship with food would follow me throughout my teens and twenties. As eating has nourished my relationships, so my not eating has threatened to sabotage them. Reading and writing about food – first for Borough Market's magazine and website, then for a whole range of magazines and newspapers – has been a large part of my recovery, and it is out of this contradiction and evolution that *Hungry Heart* has been born.

I have found food is inextricable from – even equivalent to – love, to the point where knowing where food ends and love starts feels impossible. Discussing this book with relatives and friends I've found almost everyone had an anecdote to share, a view to voice, a recipe that reminds them of a particular feeling or relationship. 'I've got a recipe from every man I ever dated,' a family friend once revealed, and while you've got to admire her zeal, you don't have to be as gastronomically thorough as that to see how your eating patterns have been shaped by a culinary composite of family, partners, colleagues, faith and friends.

Hungry Heart is not a definitive guide to food and love. Even if such a definitive guide was possible, I am neither old enough nor experienced enough in either subject to write it. Nor is this an academic book, although I have cited the odd expert where relevant to the story I'm telling. For the most part *Hungry Heart* is largely born of my experiences, interwoven with conversations I've had with friends, fellow food writers and family members along the way.

Traversing from Grandma's hotplate through my parents' divorce, I've explored the formative influence of family in what we eat, when we eat and who we tend to eat with. I've looked at friendships – for, in an age where personal and professional pressures have reduced the majority of our interactions to taking place on the Internet, we're increasingly combining IRL face time with meals. I've touched on religion: not just feasts days, which unite those with faith (and without) around the table, but tabooed foods, the sacrifice of which marks out the devout from the non-believer.

As we grow up, food becomes not just something we're dished up but something we choose for ourselves: a means of identity and self-expression akin to MacBooks, Nikes and canvas tote bags. I've tried to explore the myriad ways we find, define and relate to ourselves through food, as well as to others, and unearth why so many of us still balk at the idea of eating alone. I've looked at dating, of course – the cooking, the ordering in, the 'You have that, I insist' dance of culinary courtship that will at best end in matrimony, at worst a great anecdote. And I have tried to articulate the role food and drink play in the workplace: the strange sense of intimacy that comes with knowing your colleague's coffee order, the importance of getting a round in, and the power of a halved original glazed Krispy Kreme to transform a colleague into a friend.

It would be ambitious to the point of rank arrogance to say *Hungry Heart* is for anyone who has ever loved and eaten; I am acutely aware that my own experience is rooted in my being white, heterosexual, female and middle class, for all that I have included a variety of perspectives. Yet I hope that I have gone some way toward articulating a universality of feeling, even if I am not universal myself. When the word 'food' has come to mean so much more than food; when it comprises not just fuel and nutrients, but status, skill and identity; when our relationship toward what, when and where we eat has become ever-more complicated; the time feels ripe to cut through the clutter and ask how our meals shape our love for ourselves and other people. I hope you disagree with some of what I've said. I hope you agree with more of it. Above all, I hope you'll add your story; for if I *do* have an ambition for this book, it is to provide a feast in which readers can find and nourish themselves.

Recipe: Grandma's millionaire's shortbread

The recipe for the shortbread part of the millionaire's shortbread actually comes from Delia, who in turn credits her friend John Tovey (one of Britain's first celebrity chefs). The topping is Grandma's, though it was Grandad who took charge when it came to microwaving the condensed milk. I don't know if he did this because it was a bit dangerous; I do know that when in India in the war, he swapped his cigarette rations for cans of condensed milk, he had that much of a sweet tooth, so I suspect an ulterior motive. Spread the caramel thick, and the chocolate thin. This makes around 12 squares.

FOR THE SHORTBREAD

Ingredients
175g/6¼oz plain flour
85g/3oz caster sugar
175g/6¼oz salted butter, at room temperature
85g/3oz fine semolina

Method
Place all the ingredients in a mixing bowl and rub together until crumbly. We used a spoon when we were kids because it made us feel grown up, but you're best off using your hands. Bring together to a dough, transfer the dough to a lined square tin and press it out evenly, smoothing it with the back of a tablespoon. Prick with a fork. Bake near the centre of the oven for 1 to 1¼ hours until it is a pale gold shade. Allow the shortbread to cool in the tin for 10 minutes, then transfer to a wire rack to cool completely – don't cut it yet.

FOR THE MILLIONAIRE'S TOPPING

Ingredients
2 tbsp golden syrup
140g/5oz condensed milk
110g/3¾oz unsalted butter
55g/2oz caster sugar
200g/7oz dark chocolate (about 70% cocoa solids)

Method
Put all ingredients except the chocolate in a microwave-friendly bowl and microwave for a minute at a time, stirring each time. It should take around eight to ten minutes in total, but you need to stir and observe as you go. Watch your fingers because the mixture is very hot and sticky; famously, Grandma once dropped it all over her legs, resulting in terrible burns. The mixture will turn golden over time – you don't want it too dark, or it will split. You want it soft but firm-ish; you can test it on a saucer. Carefully pour the mixture over the cooled shortbread and leave to set as it cools while you melt the chocolate in the microwave. Spread the melted chocolate over the cooled caramel. Leave it to cool once more before cutting it into squares. Give the corner to the person who needs it most. It's okay if that's you.

1

Dad's Microwaved Scrambled Eggs

Divorce, dinners and single dads

I have very little recollection of dinners prior to my parents'
divorce – which is odd, because I was six at the time and as
divorces go, theirs was not traumatic. There was no simmering
tension at the dinner table, no throwing of plates or even
insults. Mummy and Daddy still loved each other; they just
didn't want to be together anymore, they told me at the end of
a damp holiday in Brittany.

What remains of my life 'BD' are a series of sensory
shadows: smells, mostly, like the cafetière coffee they made on
weekend mornings, or the earthy red wine and spicy Bombay
Mix they enjoyed before dinner. I'm no psychologist, but
it's interesting that my memories centre not on what I ate or
drank, but what I saw my parents share together when they
were at their most relaxed.

To this day, I regard morning coffee and pre-dinner drinks
as golden hours, in which time recentres around brewing a

cafetière, selecting a chocolate biscuit or uncorking a wine bottle. Free from the pressure placed on meals, these liminal slithers can yield the richest conversations: no one person carries the burden of preparation, there's little room for error, and no one is seeking nutritional sustenance. Because they exist solely to facilitate pleasure and communality, they inspire it, like cathedrals stirring spiritual feelings in the hearts of even the most cynical visitors. They engage all our senses: not just taste and smell, but touch, sight, sound and wonder, so that even as a child (when their headier pleasures were lost on me) I knew from the glug-glug-glug of the bottle, the resonant crunch of Bombay Mix, the firm resistance of the plunger in the flurry of coffee grains, that something good was about to take place.

I also knew, with the finely tuned antennae all children (but particularly children of divorce) carry, that it was not the same when Mum left; that these moments were more than the sum of their substances. Though Dad soldiered valiantly on with pre-dinner drinks, serving my brother and I goblets of red grape juice and clinking his wine glass with ours cheerily, it was some time before we made this ritual our own. For years after the divorce, neither Mum nor Dad bought Bombay Mix, so that the crunchy snack has become my Proustian madeleine moment. Whilst coffee and wine have since been overlain by other, stronger memories during adulthood, Bombay Mix exists in isolation: a spicy, sensory portal to the world in which my parents ate and drank together in our terraced house in west London.

Neuroscience and psychology have since corroborated that this association I have between food and my parents' marriage is unsurprising. Indeed, it is to be expected. Sandra Wheatley is a psychologist who specialises in children and divorce and she tells me that when our emotions are heightened, our memories become so clear and focused that everything – smell, taste, even colours – feels more vivid and intense. Strong emotional memories often become strong physical memories, she explains, 'and as we often have emotional discussions over food and drink, it's not surprising that food and emotion seem to go hand in hand'. At its most benign, this is why I love my grandma's millionaire's shortbread and why most of us feel a nostalgic fondness for birthday cake, or the sweets we shared as children. Yet when allied with discord, loss or even just an unpleasant bout of food poisoning, the dishes we once savoured can turn to ash in our mouths.

I am reminded of a conversation I once had with food writer Diana Henry, when she told me how her children refused to eat roast chicken at her house in the years following her divorce from their father. The simple Sunday roast chicken which had been a hallmark of their family's togetherness became the reverse when their dad served it at *his* house each Sunday, just prior to Diana arriving to pick them up. 'They called it divorce chicken,' she sighed. Though the fowl is famously Diana's favourite meat – and a roast her favourite method – Diana knew better than to force on her kids a dish so laden with sad connotations: 'I can't imagine how hard it must have been for them. Even the smell of it they couldn't stand.' Instead, she found a new chicken dish, devised by Palestinian chef Sami Tamimi and rich with spice and sumac. 'It wasn't a roast chicken from *their* past. It was a roast chicken from Sami's past, from his childhood in Palestine,' she told me. It wasn't served for Sunday lunch, but midweek for dinner. Crucially, it was part of their new family of three rather than their four-strong family of old.

Diana's 'divorce chicken' story is a vivid reminder of food's potential not just to cement old identities, but to forge new ones. It's hard to believe now, but when my parents separated in 1996, divorce was something of a rarity at my school. The only other girl in my class whose parent's had split was my friend Claudia, and neither of us spoke of it back then; it seemed almost shameful. Today, however, Claudia puts her career as a cake baker down in part to her parents' divorce. In the absence of her mum, who left in acrimonious circumstances when Claudia was very small, baking cakes for others speaks to the role she always wanted to play in the playground, in the Wendy house where we played mummies and daddies. It spoke to what she now wryly calls 'the big Jewish mother in me', who just wants to bring people together.

My dad is not a baker. He was not even much of a cook, in the years following his divorce. Like most men of his generation, his culinary skills extended to toasting and reheating. Though he loved food and, thanks to a father who travelled all over the world, had the most educated palate of anyone we knew at the time, he had no idea how to prepare it. We ate adventurously, and randomly: custard apples, Heinz soup, passion fruit, and fish in a bag. I can reliably claim we ate – and mostly disliked – avocados long before they were fashionable. Yet what mattered to Dad over and above anything he put on the table was our all being round it at the same time, to the point that even a cup of tea made on the hoof was – and is still, to our occasional, loving frustration – regarded as a communal activity.

Pre-divorce, this impulse was not apparent, yet as the dust settled into Mum's house and Dad's house, meals at Dad's took on a pseudo-religious quality. Every mealtime was sacrosanct; every meal an occasion, whether it was early morning hot chocolate – for which we sleepily snuck into his bed before school – or his infamously stiff scrambled eggs. Both were made in the microwave, the patron saint of culinary challenged fathers, but while the former was improved by the cooking method, which left fat, sweet bubbles of chocolate powder on the surface ready to burst on our tongues, the latter was not.

Whipped up with milk and microwaved until just short of solid, these were everything scrambled eggs shouldn't be: pale, dry and quivering. When Dad served them atop slices of I Can't Believe It's Not Butter-ed toast, they retained the shape of the measuring jug they were cooked in – yet we ate them without complaint. We had no point of comparison, scrambled eggs not being in our mother's culinary canon – and even if we had, we wouldn't have made one. When it came to our parents, our golden rule was to never compare. Whilst my brother Nicholas's silky soft, buttery eggs are a point of pride today, it wasn't an aversion to Dad's eggs that drove him to perfect them. 'For a long time I thought eggs were always cooked in a microwave,' he once recollected. 'That was what scrambled eggs were.'

Being a sentimental sort, I would love to attribute my brother's penchant for scrambled eggs to our father triumphing in the face of adversity to scramble our dinner together. In reality, Nicholas is a practical man who likes eggs and has learnt to perfect them. Yet there's no denying the love that went into the dishes Dad made during his shell-shocked single years. Though the phrase 'cooked with love' is a cliché bandied around everywhere from Michelin-starred restaurants to supermarkets, our dad cooked 'with love' because he had to: because love and – crucially – the microwave was really all he knew how to cook with.

Love was, if you like, his signature flavour, discernible in everything from microwaved Weetabix to Chicken Tonight. Everything we ate came with his inimitable blend of stress, expletives and care. Though dinner at Mum's was both more punctual and more competent, it was around Dad's table that we learnt when someone who loves you cooks for you, they are putting more on your plate than sustenance. We learnt that cooking is love – but so, too, is eating; that if you *do* want to be together, it doesn't matter what the food's like. And we learnt that, in the kitchen, our funny, kind, clever and in all other respects capable father was flawed.

Mouthful by mouthful, meal by meal, we discovered what many people don't learn until adulthood: your parents aren't perfect. Dad remains the most intelligent, practical man I know, able to answer any question, and translate even the most complex of K'Nex sets into fairground rides. That the most basic cookery instructions could reduce him to swearing profusely at a microwave stood us in good stead for an adult world in which most people are muddling along.

If anything, his ineptitude was endearing – for what Dad lacked in cookery knowhow he made up for in customised utensils. His love for these tools, coupled with his greedy instinct for seasonality, lent an air of festivity to certain foods throughout the year. Winter brought forth red grapefruits, cut with a grapefruit knife and served with serrated grapefruit spoons. Spring heralded asparagus and I Can't Believe It's Not Butter served with a butter knife. In June he insisted we hull strawberries with a specific strawberry huller, whilst in August corn on the cob came with crampon-like grips for its slippery pool of ICBINB. Of course, we were lucky in that Dad knew what good produce looked like, when to buy it and, crucially, was able to pay for it – a blessing we were even back then vaguely aware of. Though hardly gourmet, these entertaining, endearing jumbles of luxury and mundanity were a triumph of taste and togetherness at a time when the world felt particularly disorientating.

So we bellowed 'I Feel Like Chicken Tonight', spun riddles about ICBINB and other butter spreads and squealed in disgust when Dad revealed a grin full of corn kernels: 'Saving these for later,' he'd jest. Though dinner at Mum's was tastier and less chaotic, there was an air of collusion to these meals *à trois*: a gleeful, half devoted, half devil-may-care camaraderie that courses through our dynamic even to this day. Like the strawberry hullers and grapefruit spoons, the foundations of our relationship were laid down during those years, over that kitchen table. Love, for my dad, was cutting around the 14 segments in a grapefruit half and crowning each with a glittering pile of sugar. Love for us was eating them: scraping the flesh clean off the pith with our serrated spoons, wincing at the bitter tang, then slurping the sweet, sugary juice straight from the bowl.

Most of the time, when people ask how I came to be a food writer, I tell them about my grandma's hotel and growing up in its vast, clattering kitchen. I talk about my mum's love of literature, my work at Borough Market and the friends I have made through food. Only recently have I come to feel that my dad has had far more of an influence than I give him credit for on my career. His insatiable curiosity when it came to exotic fruits, novelty flavours of crisps or – when eating out – the dessert 'special' inspired a childlike sense of excitement around food whether we were in Tesco or our local Italian restaurant, playing with the wax on the wine bottle candle holders. Popular wisdom has it that those who work in food must have inherited their love of it through the attuned palate and good cooking of their mother or grandmother but my experience suggests it is not so much food that draws people into the industry, as the feelings around it. Claudia and I have worked in food for years now and have often observed that many in our industry have had quite traumatic childhoods, and are aiming to look after, please and be liked by feeding.

By the time we left school, the statistics had caught up with Claudia and I, and we were joined by several other children of divorced parents. Amongst them was Emma, a school friend whose parents separated when she was 19, and who has also gone on to work in food. Unlike us, Emma's parents had been together for most of her childhood and their culinary rituals, like going to the same curry house in Harrow for birthdays and celebrations, were well established and inextricably tied to their three-strong family. Thus when they eventually parted ways, meal times took on a slightly different emotional hue.

Needless to say, neither parent took Emma for curry again – at least not to *their* place, near Harrow station. Emma's mum loved eating out, and would happily whisk her off to new, exciting places in London. Yet as the injured party Emma's dad was reluctant even to leave Northwood – and our hometown was not exactly blessed with restaurants beyond Lomito's, a steak restaurant with delusions of grandeur, and Tai Pan, a pan-Asian place of faded glory. With bare cupboards at home, going to one or other was less of a treat, more of a panicked sense of 'salary, sort this out', Emma remarked once – a familiar feeling I suspect, for many single dads looking to feed their kids something other than toast.

Of course, the difference between ages 6 and 19 is substantial, particularly when it comes to the often-still-gendered roles of father and daughter. At 6, my sense of responsibility for Dad's feelings was confined to eating his food and loudly enjoying it; at 19, Emma quickly assumed a more active role. Microwave or not, scrambled eggs were not forthcoming unless Emma made them, having first asked her dad to buy the ingredients. 'That's the moment when the divorce always felt real: when I opened the fridge, and it was like – tumbleweed' Emma joked once, gesturing with her hands to illustrate said weed billowing down an empty alley. We laugh about it now, but nothing says 'your parent is struggling' more viscerally than a barren fridge when you come home.

As Sandra the psychologist points out, food can be a very physical reminder of something lost – particularly something that, under different circumstances, could have continued. Yet Emma's story also shows how that hole can be filled with new rituals for, after a year or so of playing mother and trying to 'jazz up' food at her father's, she realised it would never be the same – and that was okay. Dinner at her dad's was never going to have the sense of fanfare meals at her mum's brought, and rather than force it she decided to make peace with it. 'Now I try to keep things stress free. I pick up ham, cheese, olives and bits from Waitrose and we have a picnic in front of the telly,' she tells me. 'We had the family food identity with the curry; now Dad and I have our own food identity.'

I think about my dad with his customised cutlery, corn kernel grin, and tendency to steal mouthfuls of our chocolate gateau at ASK Italian because it was better than the more 'interesting' dessert he'd chosen. Emma is right: what children need is not just food, but a relationship through food – the cumulative, meal-based memories which make you feel part of a tribe. The problems our fathers faced, being of a generation of men who went straight from mothers to marriage, is that their food identity had been largely subsumed by their wives' food identity, which reflected that of her maiden family. As a result, our dads were left with nothing when their marriages ended. 'Assets, furniture – those we split 50:50,' my mum says, when I point this out to her. 'But recipes and food rituals can't be split, really – and most of them were mine.'

Afternoon tea with homemade cake, mid-morning coffee with chocolate biscuits, recipes for pies and puddings – all left my dad when Mum left. He hung onto tea (or hot chocolate) in bed each morning before breakfast, but the other, newer food identities he forged with us over time. Again, popular wisdom has it that families are built on handed-down dishes like roast potatoes, beef ragu, apple pie or chicken soup. Yet our microwave scrambled eggs, Emma's sofa picnic – even Claudia's dad's 'burnt Bugs Bunny', the bunny-shaped nuggets he overcooked with comforting regularity – were no less talismanic for being basic. As Emma told me, 'I like that Dad and I found our new stride.'

Meals at Mum's continued much as they had pre-divorce, my mum being – amongst many other things – the patron saint of consistency. This may sound dull next to Dad's slightly more seat-of-his-pants approach, but it wasn't. It still isn't. Consistency is, after all, a precursor of comfort and comfort is a condition of love. Mum's cooking provided clockwork beats of routine, warmth and competency at a time when my life felt anything but routine, warm or competent. Though they eventually alighted on a pattern (Mondays and Tuesdays Mum's, Wednesdays and Thursdays Dad's, weekends alternate) in those early years each week differed according to my parents' work commitments – so Nicholas and I could quite feasibly be at Dad's on Monday, Mum's on Tuesday, Dad's on Wednesday, Mum's on Thursday and Friday and then, come Saturday morning, back to the paternal half.

For a girl without any innate aptitude for organisation, this was bewildering. Not a week went by without something winding up in the wrong place: my homework, my school uniform, my tennis racket, my piano books. As a result, I lived for the predictable; for stumbling sleepily into Mum's bed first thing for a cup of tea and a CLUB biscuit, and running my fingers over it until C...L...U...B showed through the silver foil. I lived for the joke told by Simon Bates on Classic FM just after 7 a.m. – or rather, I lived for rating it with my mum and Nicholas on a scale of basic to full-body-cringeworthy. For years I insisted upon exactly the same breakfast – hot Weetabix – and I opted for packed lunch as soon as I could, just so I knew what was coming. 'Comfort food can be all sorts of things, for all sorts of reasons,' Sandra observes. 'It's not always something rich, or hot, or even something your family has made. Sometimes it's just something that makes you feel safe; something you understand.'

Like Dad, Mum placed great emphasis on the importance of our eating together, on mealtimes as a means of reconnecting not just refuelling. Mostly this is a reflection of their own upbringing – 'If you're eating, you're at the table' my grandma says, and my dad's dad would have agreed – but I also suspect this had something to do with our living with our parents only half the time. Absence makes the heart grow fonder, and the head less inclined to squander what little time you have together watching TV during dinner or skipping breakfast for a cereal bar. When we weren't playing sport, our weekends revolved around eating and drinking. During the week, once we'd grown out of the au pairs who frequented our early years, we'd hold out for dinner until our parents came home. Indeed, such was our anxiety to eat with our parents we'd sometimes have two meals: one after school to tide us over, and another upon their arrival. 'I couldn't believe how late you were going to bed some nights,' says my stepmum now, recalling Nicholas and I bleary-eyed, stomachs rumbling in unison, waiting for the sound of Dad's key in the door.

Today, friends would probably describe my need to eat *with* people as bordering on pathological. I cannot start until everyone else's food has arrived. I cannot finish until the last person puts down their fork. I cannot eat out on my own. Whoever I'm living with, the first words on my lips are 'What's the plan today?' and by plan, I invariably mean, 'When and where are our meals?' Claudia tells me she's the same. 'If someone wants to do something, I'm like "Okay what meal are we talking",' she laughs. 'If people come here and I don't have food in, it makes me really upset. Even if they're just popping in for tea, I'll have to go and get some biscuits. When you have something you enjoy you want to share it with people – so of course it makes sense to me to share food.'

In short, divorce has indelibly shaped our relationship to food, and to others through food – sometimes for the worse, but mostly for the better. This is by no means a given, as I'm reminded when asking friend and food writer Bee Wilson about her experience of divorced parents and food. When her dad left, her mum stopped cooking for them altogether. 'It was like cooking was just for men,' she recalls, and the realisation at just 14 that their mother wasn't going to cook for them any more paved the way for her and her sister to struggle with eating. Bee also – in her book *First Bite*, which is all about children and eating behaviours – recalls vividly how her dad would send her back to her mum's house after visits with a magazine and a large box of Maltesers for the train.

Not until she had children herself did Bee realise the emotional value of food is often two sided and that her dad also sought solace in giving her treats for the train. 'By casting himself as the bringer of treats, the generous provider, he could make goodbyes less painful for him as well as for me,' she writes insightfully in *First Bite*. In the short term this exchange worked. Bee got her sugar, her dad got his endorphins. Long term, however, this meant that for years afterward Bee could hardly contemplate boarding a train without something sweet in hand, be it a biscuit, pastry or hot chocolate. It was, like those sweet, airy Maltesers themselves, a semi-hollow victory that left both parties feeling dissatisfied long term.

In short, post-divorce, even food given in the hope of inciting pleasure can feel laced with pain if it doesn't reflect or result in a genuine connection. Diana vividly recalls her failed efforts to use mealtimes to bond with her new (and now ex) partner's children after their respective divorces. 'They came every Wednesday and every other weekend, and I thought food was the way I tried to pull everyone together. I thought we could be happy at the table. But it didn't work, because they didn't want to be there – because even though I wasn't the reason their dad split up with their mum, it felt like it to them.' By playing with their phones and refusing to engage over dinner, the children quietly declared their allegiance to their mum, and rejection of Diana. Given their respective cooking abilities, this feels a tragi-comic inverse of my brother and I eagerly eating my dad's microwaved scrambled eggs to affirm our allegiance to him.

Food is never just food. Cooking is never just cooking. It is an exchange between eater and cook, and the message can often get lost in translation. Nowhere in the world is this more viscerally obvious than in the broken family home, where at times every mouthful can feel heavy with meaning. When that exchange lands however, it is a joy: a pale, pepper-flecked joy, quivering and jiggling upon buttered toast at the table. These are the meals that heal and unite – and lay the foundation for better things.

Recipe: Dad's Microwaved Scrambled Eggs

'Well, it's not really a recipe,' Dad says when I ask him, as if I hadn't since figured out that like most single dads of his generation, he was constantly improvising. Still, all credit to the man, he can remember it, though he encourages readers to tweak to their own tastes. For my own part, I encourage readers to skip straight to Delia Smith, and her reassuringly stove-based recipe in *How to Cook, Book One*.

Ingredients, for three hungry people
8 eggs
30–45ml/1–1½fl oz milk
Pinch of cracked black pepper
Pinch of paprika

Method
Crack the eggs into a measuring jug along with the other ingredients. Whisk up with a fork or an actual whisk, if you're feeling cheffy. Put in microwave on medium to high power for 60–90 seconds. Remove and stir well, and microwave for another 60–90 seconds. Keep doing this until it's how you like it – or rather, just short of how you like it, as it will continue to cook after you take it out.

2

Melanie's Rice Pudding

For the love of – and in – kitchens

'So what do you think of Melanie?' my dad ventured one night, perching tentatively on the edge of my bed as I lay reading. I put down my latest instalment of *Animorphs*, feeling for once that it's humans-mutating-into-animals-to-fight-aliens drama might be eclipsed by something in real life. Though no explicit reference had been made to the fact Melanie and my dad were 'dating', from the moment we met her and her sons Alexander and Angus in Bekonscot Model Village it was obvious this was more than a friendship. Dad hadn't made new friends since Mum left. With two kids and a demanding job as a City solicitor, he barely had time to see the friends he had already. Melanie was smart, attractive, as zany as my father and yet 'cool' at the same time. Her boys were adorable without being anodyne. In not so many words, I conveyed as much to my dad.

'Oh, jolly good darling,' he said, his relief glowing in the lamplight. 'So you wouldn't mind if they came to live with us?'

I beamed in response because for, as long as I could recall, I'd been a big family girl trapped in a small – and, post-divorce, diminished – family. The idea of rambunctious meals around our currently needlessly long pine table, warmed by Melanie's food and our leaking oven, filled me with something deeper than joy. The much-touted truism that you are only as happy as your least happy child often cuts both ways in my case, and until he met Melanie, my dad had not really been happy. Much as I loved our meals *à trois*, I was acutely aware that our Chicken Tonight and microwaved eggs were not filling his emotional hole.

So Melanie came, along with her boys, her golf clubs, her Princess Di glamour and her determination to 'feed your father up' stirred into Bolognese or rice pudding. I remember the blistering, brown skin of the latter: bizarre and utterly repulsive to a child used to the bland, sweet slop of Ambrosia. 'It's the best bit,' Melanie would say, peeling it off like a sun burn and nibbling contentedly. Beneath it lay the good stuff: velvety, creamy, plump rice studded with plumper raisins, the scent somehow instantly nostalgic for the big family I'd recently acquired. Today rice pudding feels like the dish that forged us: the squeals over the skin, the jostling for the jam jar, the stolen mouthfuls from the fridge the next morning talismanic of our collective identity.

Melanie and my dad got married soon after, and she and the boys moved in, in a ceremony that was in almost all respects conventional. There was a church service, speeches, a white dress and a cake which my aunt baked and drove nervously around the M25 with a handwritten sign stuck to the rear that said, 'cake on board'. Our surnames, however, remained unchanged. Melanie, Alexander and Angus were Hamilton; Dad, Nicholas and me were Finney in a break with tradition about which there was no consultation – at least not with us kids – and which disproportionately irked me. To my mind, Alexander and Angus *were* my brothers, in all but name and genetic material. The latter, no one could help; the former seemed needless to the mind of a child who craved consistency, in spirit and name.

Deep down I understood that Hamilton linked the boys to their father, Finney linked us to our mum, and of course, Melanie and my dad wanted the same name as their respective children. Nevertheless, in the absence of nominative evidence, I cleaved to concrete signs of our being *whole*. Foremost amongst these was our kitchen table: a soft, warm pine number pockmarked with mug rings, which Melanie sat at one end, flanked by her children; and Dad at the other, flanked by Nicholas and me. No matter what meal it is or how many guests we have, this seating plan remains unchanged. Even when it's just Melanie and my dad at dinner they sit in the same places, holding forth across the clutter of bills, legal papers, *The Times* and water glasses stuffed with garden flowers. As such, this table unites the two families regardless of who's at home.

Most tables tell tales. Kitchen tables keep time, like insentient sentinels charting the presence and preoccupations of their charges. Even today, the best way of telling who's home at my dad's is to head to the kitchen and survey the table scene. You'll know from which mugs have been used, and which magazines are open at which pages. You'll know from Melanie's reminders, penned on the back of envelopes and left in the place of whoever it is she wants to communicate with. You'll see her in the soaking porridge pan, detect Angus in lingering vegan bacon aroma, Nicholas in the smell of scrambled eggs and Dad from the disarray of documents – though you will have been alerted to his presence long before that by the inimitable sound of his sneeze.

Mostly, though, you'll know because the kitchen is where you're most likely to find us: locating a charger, making a cuppa or warming our backs on the leaky oven. 'If you want life, go to the kitchen,' my mum once observed of my grandma's kitchen, and the observation holds true of kitchens more generally. To paraphrase the late, great writer Laurie Colwin, in a kitchen, you are never truly alone. 'Even at her most solitary, a cook in the kitchen is surrounded by generations of cooks past, the advice and menus of cooks present, the wisdom of cookbook writers,' Colwin writes in her seminal book, *Home Cooking*. For all that ready meals and takeaways might make cooking redundant, the kitchen has retained its totemic importance. It is the checking in point, to which visitors and family alike head to on arrival. It is a hive of activity and a dumping ground for anything and everything.

I think about all the kitchens I've known in my life, from my grandparent's hotel to my flat in North London. All have exhibited these cosy, communal characteristics, albeit to greatly varying degrees. Though beautiful in glass and chrome, the kitchen Mum had when we were teenagers never stirred the same feelings as that at Dad's – mainly because the design inhibited them. The table was glass and hidden from the entrance; the fridge was too tucked away for a fly-by Frube or fridge-cold plum, and the imposingly gleaming kitchen island seemed to barricade the entrance. You couldn't mingle, much less dump, flop or steal a fistful of cereal – and as a consequence, the kitchen was not a place in which we'd convene.

Mum knew this – and when she moved, it was getting the kitchen 'right' that she most cared about. Yet what is it that makes a kitchen the heart of the household? It's not the size or the stylishness, for even the smallest, shabbiest kitchens can exude a certain magnetism; nor is it necessarily the food. During the lockdowns of 2020 and 2021 – and beyond, with the meteoritic rise in home working – many of us thought long and hard about our homes, as we were spending so much time inside them. It was in writing about what this would mean for our kitchens that I came across acclaimed kitchen designer Johnny Grey.

Grey is, it is safe to say, no run of the mill kitchen designer. For one thing, he grew up with the now iconic cookery writer Elizabeth David as a close family friend. When his mother took her own life – when Grey was just eight years old – she stepped in to help his father and younger siblings. His father cooked on occasion – 'He did a cookery course when our mother died and came away with a book called *101 Ways to Cook an Egg*,' Grey smiles – but for the most part it was Grey who cooked, with David hovering in the background. 'I think I knew that food and mealtimes were key to holding life together – and pleasure, too,' he explains.

Grey's philosophy is simple, informed by his formative childhood as well as by the disciplines of neuroscience and sociology. He tells me the potted history of kitchens: how, from the industrial revolution onwards, they stopped being inclusive, communal areas – at least in cities; farmhouse kitchens, being necessary to a family's economic life as well their social one, remained largely unchanged. 'The industrial revolution happened in just 30 years in the UK. In France it's taken over 150 years, and it's still going on. It wasn't intentional, but such rapid industrialisation, particularly of food, destroyed many of our domestic habits,' Grey continues. 'No domestic culture can survive that pace of change.'

The less time we spent in our urban kitchens, the more functional they became, the more they turned into 'slave-like holes for women to do their "duty" in.' Farmhouse kitchens, meanwhile, continued to be places 'where all people and activities were welcomed' – hence, perhaps, the rustic ideals attached to Agas and vintage blue and white plates. Inspired by this history and by more recent research around our relationship to rooms and objects, Grey came to feel the ideal kitchen was not just somewhere to eat and prepare food in, but a third place, which is neither the home nor the office; a place that channels the conviviality and happy bustle of the farmhouse kitchen, and makes you feel rooted and safe.

In designing his kitchens, Grey puts safety first – not just the practical aspects, but the *feelings* of safety generated by light, space and warmth. Kitchen preparation areas which face a wall or an extractor fan are the worst, he says, because if your peripheral vision is interrupted, it will prompt a 'fight or flight' response. Repositioning those areas to enable eye contact with your guests 'can trigger behaviour that stimulates the production of oxytocin or serotonin, which is what you want when preparing food or eating together,' he explains simply. 'Preparing food was an act of love for me as a young person looking after my family – and it is now. I want to design kitchens that encourage people to spend as much time doing that as they want and are able to do.'

The same goes for seating – which explains why the banquettes always fill up faster than chairs in restaurants: 'You feel safe because your back is protected, and you're not exposed to the unknown.' Grey's mission is to encourage us to pay attention to our tables, chairs and cookers, and consider the feelings and habits they inspire. 'We spend more time in the kitchen than we do anywhere else. It is the room that has the most potential for delivering happiness' he continues, citing a study by happiness economist Lord Richard Layard who found our mood lifts around breakfast and midday, and that we are in general happiest between 7 p.m. and 10 p.m. 'These are the times you are most likely to be in the kitchen, and with the people you love.'

I think warmly of my seat at the table at Dad's, backed up against the radiator and facing my brother. I think of the micro-rituals we developed in that kitchen: of Angus wearing his grapefruit goggles to stop the juice getting in his eyes; Nicholas taking so long to butter his bread and arrange his ham that we've finished lunch before he's even started; Alexander meticulously making salad dressing in the ancient dressing shaker, because he's the only one who can get the balance bang on. Separately, they don't sound like much; cumulatively, however, they weave a web of togetherness, reinforcing through repetition our identity as a family.

After all, what are relationships, if not an accumulation of anecdotes and rituals? And what could provide a more fertile ground for anecdote and ritual than food and its preparation? As Margaret Visser, the anthropologist who literally wrote the book on *The Rituals of Dinner* observed: 'a meal can be thought of as a ritual and a work of art, with limits laid down, desires aroused and fulfilled, enticements, variety, patterning and plot.' We are what we eat; not just in the nutritional sense, but in the narrative sense too. Our food becomes us. At my dad's we have forged out of six people, four gene pools and two single parents a family who eat breakfast at 1 p.m., dinner at 10 p.m. and forgets the braised red cabbage reheating in the microwave every time we have a roast.

This is not to say mealtimes at Mum's were any less meaning-ful, but they were shorter and less chaotic; less happened during dinner. Our relationship with our stepfather, David, whilst every bit as nourishing as our relationship with Melanie, was forged more through long walks and deep talks than it was by food. As a foursome, we've found our identity in food only relatively recently: Mum's had more time to cook, we eat the same food more often, and the kitchen in her current house is a homely room complete with comfy chairs and toasty Aga. It's a far cry from the old place with the obstructive worktop and glass table on which we could neither lean, cradling a cuppa, or clutter up with life's extraneous stuff.

'The old kitchen was beautiful, but there was nothing to congregate around. You need that, in a kitchen,' Mum observes when we reflect on their differences. Sometimes this is simply a person. There's no big table in Grandma's post-hotel kitchen, no range cooker or inviting island. Rather, it is Grandma herself that centres us, and draws our attention in. Her stories, her bustle, the constant cooking to 'help' with (read: pick and nibble at) combine to create a familial focal point such that all of us eventually end up in her kitchen. In Mum's new kitchen, this focal point is the Aga; a big, red, back-warming cliché of comfort underneath which the dog sits, and against which whoever is at home leans, talking, stirring and checking the timer on Siri.

Sandra, the psychologist, says this often comes down to warmth: warmth of feeling, but also literal temperature, she says. 'There is a direct relationship between feeling warm and being satisfied; between warmth and mental wellbeing. In the kitchen, you often feel warm because the oven is on, the kettle is boiling or there's something simmering on the stove.' She describes baking cakes at university; how the activity and the warmth of the oven would bring her housemates into the kitchen, where they'd chat whilst the thick batter rose, breathed in and blushed golden. Feeling warm invariably means feeling safe; feeling safe invites honesty; honesty fosters love and a sense of connection. It is a direct and telling inversion to Yoda's infamous quote about fear leading to anger, hate and the dark side.

The wonderful irony of kitchens being seen as safe havens is that they are literally brimming with danger. It is so commonplace that we don't stop to think about it, but to be with other people around kettles, cookers, knives, even cans of kidney beans is to render ourselves vulnerable. Our using these tools to nourish rather than maim our companions is a marker of civilisation. However subconsciously, it is a meaningful choice. Margaret Visser wrote in *The Rituals of Dinner* that eating is 'aggressive by nature, and the implements required for it could quickly become weapons. Table manners are, most basically, a system of taboos designed to ensure that violence remains out of the question.' Yet in the kitchen, cooking together or leaning on the counter, wine in hand, you're engaging with these potential weapons before you even get to the table and its requisite manners.

In the same way that it is easier to talk about things when you're driving, so it is easier to talk when you are side by side cooking together, says Sandra. The intermittency of eye contact plus the act of creating something together is 'a massive tick in the box for conversation – unless the conversation takes a dramatic turn, in which case put the knives down!' She is joking, though only partly. Her observation is but an extreme example of how kitchens can mirror as well as make our relationships. 'The fact someone matters is written into every move, rather than having to be spelt out explicitly. The preparation, the washing up, the putting away – even the choosing of the food, can all be tokens of love.'

Ask me for an image that illustrates my dad's relationship with my brothers, and I'll show you them washing up together after dinner. My part in the meal is over by this point, but it's worth staying in the kitchen to listen to them larking about. Sometimes they'll continue a conversational strand from dinner, taking it into an abstract, cerebral territory which Melanie, Alexander and I have no time for. Often, they'll play music, or try to sing terrible pop lyrics in schoolboy French or Spanish. '*Tu le dis mieux, quand tu ne dis rien*,' they'll warble, laughing, as Dad washes and Angus and Nicholas dry and put away in smooth tandem.

There's an intimacy to this image which, like cooking together, contains an almost dance-like quality. As anyone who has watched an elderly couple on the dancefloor knows, the more established and comfortable the relationship, the better and more enjoyable the dance. Over many meals and stacks of dirty dishes, Dad, Angus and Nicholas have built a level of trust and understanding that is manifest in their synchronicity around the sink and the dishwasher. My dad is not a man given to explicitly expressing his pleasure in the company of others, but his happiness is palpable when he's butchering Ronan

Keating in Franglaise whilst passing hot, soapy wine glasses to the boys to dry.

Of course, the power of cooking and food to forge and maintain connections within families necessarily extends well beyond the domestic kitchen. Never was this more obvious than during the pandemic, when family members estranged by the lockdowns exchanged recipes, food and photos of food. Social distance made our hearts grow fonder and our appetites keener. Throughout spring and summer 2020 Nicholas, Mum and I rang Grandma to ask for her cooking advice, we baked her hot cross buns, millionaire's shortbread and Yorkshires and sent pictures. Yet for the many millions of people who, for whatever reason, no longer live in the same country as their families, cooking to connect to one's relatives is nothing new.

I've lost count of the number of chefs and food writers who have made their names championing the cuisine of their homeland, but say they only got into cooking after leaving it for Britain. Asma Kahn is a case in point. Shortly after arriving here as a lawyer alongside her new husband, she flew back to India to learn how to cook from her mum because she was 'homesick, unhappy, hungry and cold.' Today Asma is one of the most acclaimed chefs in Britain. Her London restaurant, Darjeeling Express, has been featured from *Sunday Brunch* to Netflix's *Chef's Table*. Yet that yearning for family, continuity and connection is the spirit in which Asma runs her all-female kitchen, with love, justice – everyone is paid the same hourly rate – and a biryani famed for making Indian guests cry.

I myself have not cried over Asma's biryani, but that isn't to say it's wonder is lost on me. Though it is just one of thousands, if not hundreds of thousands of family biryani recipes in India, it evokes the same feelings in her guests as if it were their own family recipe, passed down their maternal line. It's as if I were to eat someone else's grandma's millionaire's shortbread and feel the same sense of comfort as I do eating *my* grandma's shortbread, the shortbread robust, the caramel fudgy with condensed milk. It seems impossible. Yet Asma tells me her biryani's power has less to do with the recipe, more with the way it is cooked.

'The women who cook in my kitchen – they all come from a tradition of cooking family recipes, with love, patience and time. Time is the most expensive ingredient.' Anything else in the dish – rice, spices, even meat – can be bought; time alone is irreplaceable. This is true of all home cooking, but it is particularly true of those dishes which take hours, even days to prepare; that are cooked entirely from scratch. 'The layering, the delicacy, the aromas, the patience; time is what you pour of yourself into that dish,' Asma continues, 'and that time becomes a homage. You can see it in the eyes of the cooks, and you can taste it.' It's almost too obvious and it's certainly in line with this book's premise, but the reason Asma's biryani inspires the same degree of feeling in her guests as their family's biryani is simply because it is prepared with the same degree of care and love.

Part of me longs to experience the same bittersweet feelings of comfort as Asma's Indian guests do upon eating her biryani. The other, more sombre part of me knows the precursor to this kind of comfort is suffering; that the emotional significance of this dish is derived from loss and separation; and that for as long as my mum's cheesy pasta is 85 miles in one direction and my grandma's caramel shortbread 60 miles in the other, variations of either are unlikely to bring tears to my eyes.

Indeed, I would even go so far as to say that one of the defining features of comfort food *is* distance, of time or space, and that it is from crossing those divisions that the food derives its power: connecting us, via our senses, to the feeling of being cared for.

My friend Viv moved to the UK from Australia aged just 22 and has been an enviably capable cook for as long as I've known her. When I wrote earlier of the magnetism of small kitchens, it was chiefly hers I was thinking of: a narrow galley kitchen in faded white, with a fridge at the end around which – come the deservedly legendary house parties she throws with her husband Jon – we all cram. Viv's roast cauliflower with tahini is a revelation: charred, crispy, fudgy and drenched with crushed sesame seeds, it's one of a number of dishes she is known for. I am not surprised in the slightest when Viv tells me the kitchen is one of the few places she's always felt confident; that, 10,500 miles away from her homeland, she found connection in cooking for people and using food to show her new friends that she cared.

What I had not known, prior to asking her, was the extent to which this small kitchen connected Viv to her mum in Australia – during lockdowns certainly, but even prior to that, in her relaxed, recipe-free approach to rustling up dinner. When Viv tells me her mum taught her everything she knows about cooking, she doesn't mean specific techniques or even beloved family staples, but 'the art of opening the fridge and unfolding a meal'. At the heart of this art is a holistic approach to the kitchen, she explains: maintaining a well-filled cupboard, a fridge of fresh vegetables and a belief that above all else food is to be enjoyed rather than stressed over. 'In this way she has taught me everything of value and also nothing of specificity,' Viv continues – bar her exhortation to always use cheese liberally.

Viv and I talk a lot about food, but this particular discussion takes place in early 2022, toward the end of the pandemic. After two years, three London lockdowns and endless, extensive travel restrictions between the UK and Australia, Viv has finally made it back to her mum's in Sydney in time for her and Jon's long-awaited wedding. She tells me how, as the lockdowns wore on, food became a connection to home more than ever before – to the point where she even started cooking a few dishes from her early childhood, such as an Australian 'burger with the lot' – a beef burger with bacon, a fried egg, lettuce, tomato, pickled beetroot, a slice of tinned pineapple and tomato sauce. Viv can hear her mum cooking dinner as we speak, 'figuring it out based on whatever's there, as always' whilst she sits on the back veranda talking about love, cooking and kitchens. Our conversation ends with Viv being called for dinner and her heading into the kitchen she grew up in, telling me she feels 'something she hasn't felt in a long, long time: home.'

Recipe: Melanie's rice pudding

Straightforward, direct, and deeply comforting – it's funny how sometimes a recipe can completely encapsulate a person. This is a rice pudding without pomp, ceremony or accoutrements. It is rice pudding to please and to feed. You don't have to eat the skin – I never do – but you'd be surprised by how many people do actually like it. Similarly, I love it when Melanie puts raisins in and they plump up with sweet milk until they are almost grape like, but many other people find the prospect utterly repellent. You do you.

Ingredients, for six
1.1l/2pt whole milk
100g/3½oz pudding rice
75g/2¾oz sugar (granulated is fine)
Sprinkle of nutmeg
Knob of butter

Method
Bung the milk, pudding rice and sugar into a casserole dish. Top with a grating of nutmeg and a knob of butter. Cook slow – fan 130°C/150°C/gas 2 for around 2 hours – then test to see if it's ready. It should have a brown, slightly puffy skin.

3

Mum's Cheesy Pasta

A mother's love at mealtimes

In the summer of 2013, I had my first 'proper' breakup; the sort of breakup that has you balled up on the floor, wracked with sobs so intense you feel you might *literally die*. As soon as I could speak, I phoned my brother. An hour later, he was at the door of my flat: a knight in a white Citreon, ready to take me and my broken heart home.

After a pit stop at the pub and a bracing bucket of rosé, we got back to an empty house, Melanie, my dad and the boys being out for the evening. 'I thought I'd make cheesy pasta,' Nicholas announced, dumping my bag on the kitchen table and retrieving butter, pasta and a packet of Tickler Extra Mature from his own. For the first time in the 24 hours since I'd been dumped, I felt I might be alright – and, as the scent of freshly grated cheese and the sizzle of melting butter filled the air, that feeling crystalised. I was heartbroken, but I was not unloved.

Cheesy pasta is not macaroni cheese. Nor does it bear relation to anything you'll find in Italy. On the contrary, I suspect that if the dish was to get within 100 miles of the Italian border, it would be beaten back by an army of nonnas, scandalised by its unholy combination of frozen veg and Cheddary white sauce. Nevertheless, it is one of the defining dishes of my childhood for, if cheesy pasta was on the menu, it meant Mum was cooking. It meant that she both cared deeply, and that she fundamentally couldn't be bothered. It meant it was the weekend – Sunday evening, probably – and she was at ease.

When I told her this recently, she was mortified at what my favourite dish said about her cooking and inevitably, for the two remain inextricable, mothering. Yet the more I've thought and talked about it, the more I've realised that the charm of this meal was simply its simplicity and the fact we were eating it with her and David, not on our own. During the week, meals at Mum's arrived courtesy of my grandma, who loaded the boot with frozen home cooking each time we visited. For most of our childhood we had au pairs, who would ferry us between Dad's house and Mum's house and defrost Grandma's casseroles, pies and pasties each evening. These meals reverberated with her love, even whilst we ate them in her absence and the absence of our mum, who would eat an exhausted bowl of cereal when she got home from work later. Even so, a measure of how much eating *with* my mum mattered to me was that I would invariably have a second, smaller dinner alongside her on the sofa, replicating precisely Mum's combination of bran flakes, fresh fruit and Müller Light yoghurt, and sharing in her excitement about whatever fruit was in season: strawberries, Victoria plums, russet apples and the navel oranges, which, on account of her eczema, I assumed responsibility for peeling.

Come the weekend however, mealtimes were Mum's domain; a time for her to take off her business hat and pick up her battered, batter-spattered copies of Nigella, Delia or Claire Macdonald. Sometimes she relished the process, and we relished the results; other times, she simply wanted to bung something on, sit down with a glass of wine and play cards. Cheesy pasta was a meal for those times. There was no worrying if it would work out, if we'd eat it, or if it would satisfy us: we'd eat it every day if we could. Mum could spend hours slaving over salmon en croûte, and it wouldn't be met with nearly as warm a reception as the bright nuggets of peas and sweetcorn nestled within cheese-swaddled shells.

I used to feel bad about this; now I regard it fondly as testimony to the role emotion plays in a meal's enjoyment. To quote Bee Wilson, 'In those magical moments where a parent can let themselves off the hook, the child can sense that – and feels deeply happy and relaxed. We know that a child's wellbeing correlates with a mother's wellbeing from birth onwards – which is why feeling at ease is so important at the table.' Slaving over a meal for hours only to be met with indifference or, worse, disdain does more harm on both sides than good.

Those meals which are not ready meals but are not elaborate either – the beans on toasts, stuffed jacket potatoes, omelettes and so on – create a middle ground for mothers to feed their children without fuss, guilt or fear of rejection. They are the universally loved and woefully underappreciated genre of dishes my mum calls 'easy teas'. Melanie calls them 'using up dinners', which means a melange of leftovers from last night, the night before and anything approaching its use-by date. Other terms I've heard are bits-and-bobs, brown food, and – my personal favourite – 'mum bungs'. This last one comes from Polly Russell, a food historian who likens feeding her three children day in day out to 'running a small restaurant with no profit and average reviews'.

Though Polly works in food and loves cooking, there is a tyrannical quality to cooking for her kids that comes not so much from them, as from her own self-imposed pressure to care through cooking. 'I love it, I'm interested, I care, but there's a seething resentment beneath the surface,' she confesses. Her mum bungs are beloved by them all because 'they mean I can't be arsed, and they know it – but they would rather we laugh about it and eat cheese on toast, and I be in a decent mood.'

I say this tyranny is self-imposed; it is of course almost inevitable that loving a child and feeding a child should feel inextricable to its mother. From the moment of a child's conception, feeding him or her is the mother's responsibility. Within an hour of being born, they are – all being well – at their mother's breast. This intimate act, new mums are repeatedly told, is vital not just for the child's health, but for the bond between mother and baby, with breastfeeding stimulating the release of oxytocin, the famous 'love hormone'. At no point in our lives is the feeling of love so synonymous with feeding or is the emotion so united with its physical expression. Forget music, it's breastmilk that is, truly, the food of love.

At least, that's the ideal scenario, sold to pregnant women, new mothers and society in general via medics and the media. The reality for those women who, for various reasons, struggle to breastfeed is rather less rosy – as my mum found out when I was born. Her eczema rendered this 'bonding experience' excruciating, leaving her in tears and me in tears, stressed by her distress. The only thing that made the recommended minimum of two weeks' breastfeeding bearable was reading *The Forsyte Saga*, a dynastic series by John Galsworthy. To this day it is a family joke that for Mum, the mark of a good book is if she thinks it could have got her through breastfeeding me. Yet the disconnect between the image of breastfeeding she'd been presented with – mother and child with beatific expressions, entwined in a moment of perfect, peaceful union – and what she went through wasn't funny at all.

'They never show you pictures of mums crying in pain or babies unable to latch on or anything like that,' she reflects. 'You're led to believe it'll be easy for everyone; then there I was with me crying, and you crying, whilst the woman in the bed next to me could have fed the whole ward.' The idea that breastfeeding like this served to bond us seems ludicrous. On the contrary, Mum feels that carrying on under those conditions would have harmed our relationship more than enriched it. Of course, you could argue that love kept her going – but when I ask her, I learn it was less love, more fear of approbation. 'I stopped when the GP gave me permission, which is more than NCT ever would!' she exclaims of the National Childbirth Trust, the home of pre- and antenatal classes, and I am struck by the extent to which the institution made her feel that failing to breastfeed meant failing as a mum.

Thirty years later I found myself drawing upon my mum's experience to console my friend Jos, as she struggled to breast-feed her son thanks to her mastitis and his tongue-tie. Yet where my mum had jumped gratefully at the GP's permission to stop after two weeks, Jos insisted on breastfeeding for a full year – an insistence she later realised was rooted in her memories of her own parents, whom she lost before Jack was born. 'I visited a women's health carer for something like a counselling session, and she observed that my life growing up had been so deeply rooted in food. The importance of good food was something that connected me to my parents. That's why I needed to feed him; I needed to feed him to make him part of that family life that predated him,' she recalls. Like the recipe for cottage pie that Jos's mum made with her, and which she would go on to make with Jack in the same plain brown, stained pie dish, breastfeeding Jack felt like a through-line of love from her mum.

This is not, obviously, a book about breastfeeding, a subject of which I have no knowledge and even less experience; but it is a book about love, and why feeding plays such a big part of it. If it is at our mothers' breasts that we first sense this connection, then it is there too that we experience its complications: the primal instinct that clings on even when infant death becomes a more remote possibility; the implicit – and explicit – assumption that a mother's love is inextricably bound with how and what she feeds her child; the model set by our own mums, and the easy warmth and affection that can arise when both mother and child feel at ease in each other's presence.

Which brings me back to that cheesy pasta: studded with sweetcorn, flecked with mustard and served in deep, sturdy white earthenware bowls, the sight and feel of which were always instantly comforting. Though Mum has mixed feelings about our devotion to this dish today, she confesses that she didn't much think about it at the time. Like many working mums of her generation, she was too busy climbing the career ladder, smashing the glass ceiling and renovating the space beyond for me and other women of successive generations to follow her. What mattered most was that we were happy, healthy and together; and whilst sometimes that meant a full roast dinner followed by Claire Macdonald's plum cream pudding, sometimes it meant mixing frozen peas into a white sauce.

I remind her of this no-nonsense approach to our nutrition, and she laughs. 'It's hard to believe now,' she says, 'but back then there just wasn't the same level of obsession with food or identity when it came to feeding your children. We didn't read books or talk about it; we just got on with it' – a take which is echoed by other mums of her generation. My friend Eleanor's mum, Faith, also worked full-time, and calls her approach to feeding her kids 'Putting the best stuff in front of them as was possible within the remit of what they'd eat.'

She drew a line at ready meals, but wouldn't – and couldn't, being a director of planning policy in Guernsey's government – go out of her way to lavish care on a dinner Eleanor and her brother might pick around with. She bought the best quality she could afford – 100% beef burgers, 100% fish fishfingers, wholemeal bread for the packed lunches and so on – and she doesn't recall feeling bad even when, at the end of each term, she'd fish out uneaten sandwiches from the bottom of their bags. 'Perhaps it says something about me as a mother that I only emptied their rucksacks at the end of each term,' she laughs, 'but if I'm honest, I don't really recall feeling guilty. At the time, I had too much going on.'

There's an authenticity to this which I love; an authenticity echoed in Eleanor's relationship with her mother, which is not perfect but is rooted in realism. Like me, Eleanor recalls wishing her mum would collect her from school, bake cupcakes with her, be more like the mums her friends had. Like me, she learnt to love her mum not for the mum she wasn't, but for the mum she was. I remember the handful of times I'd insist on Mum baking with me, reaching for the sort of recipe that makes parents everywhere recoil – the Willy Wonka's Nutty Crunch Surprise from Roald Dahl's *Revolting Recipes* for example – and campaigning piteously until she relented. It was never the warm, loving experience I'd envisaged: not because Mum doesn't like baking, but because the chaos that inevitably ensued (as I sent lumps of sticky flapjack flying, spilled oats onto the floor and wept over the concrete block that emerged 20 minutes later) was stressful for a woman who prides herself on efficiency, efficacy and cleaning up as she goes along.

To expect her to be otherwise would be to expect her to be someone other than my devoted, but driven and pragmatic mother – and there would be little joy for either of us in her subsuming her identity. As my friend Lauren once observed of her mum, who cut countless corners whilst cooking for her three children, to what extent should you force someone to do something that doesn't come naturally to them? Lauren and her mum bonded in other ways, chiefly through fabrics and sewing: an activity which has gone on to inform Lauren's career as a sustainable fashion journalist and author. Likewise, my mum and I had plenty to bond over beyond making flapjacks, and her professional ambition and love of reading were formative in my own vocation.

In later years, once I could keep time with her rapid, busy movements and master the art of washing up as I went, I could help Mum cook; and now we love the steady patter of chopping and chatter. That, and the hours we spend walking together – either physically or on the phone – is when we have some of our most meaningful conversations; sharing, questioning, conceding and uniting whilst we peel, knead and fry. Yet I would not have had this during childhood at the expense of all that we gained thanks to her career as a communications director, and her cheesy pasta and reluctance to spend Saturdays baking are flipsides of that same coin.

None of this is to detract from the love of mothers who didn't work full-time, who did spend hours cooking for or with their kids – or indeed from the love of mums who did neither. It is more to point out how reductive and even downright misleading food is as a measure of a mother's love. When I mention this during a call with Diana Henry – the multi-award-winning writer of countless recipe columns and cookbooks, lest we forget – she is taking fish fingers out the oven for her 17-year-old son. 'I've been researching my next book all day. Why would I do anything more complicated?' she says simply. She recalls receiving a letter from a reader who said she was feeding her kids cereal and spaghetti hoops on rotation because she was grieving. 'I said to her, "It doesn't matter a damn. I'm a food writer and the thing I've cooked most for my kids is tuna, pasta and sweetcorn." I think the conflation between cooking and taking care of people can be used as a terrible stick to beat people with,' she continues, passionately – 'particularly women.'

By Diana's measure, there was more love in what Lauren's mum called her 'Friday risotto' – a melange of microwaveable rice, tinned ratatouille and frozen peas – than there was in the gravy she painstakingly made from scratch when her mother-in-law harangued her out of her Bisto habit one memorable Sunday. Indeed the example is instructive, for where the Friday risotto was always jubilantly received, the gravy went down the drain, Lauren's mum having distractedly forgotten to put a bowl in the sink when she went to sieve out the giblets. By aiming for perfection, she ended up with nothing but shame and the inedible giblets, staring accusingly at her from the sieve as they shook off the last of their gravy. It doesn't take a psychoanalyst to observe that Bisto would have been better for all concerned; that Lauren's mum was right to eschew perfection in favour of 'good enough'.

The theory of the 'good enough mother' was developed by the British psychologist Donald Winnicott, who observed that the good enough mother caters entirely to her child at first, then increasingly compromises as her child becomes less dependent, and more able to cope with her failure. In culinary terms, I think that as our ability to deal with our parents' imperfections increases, so does our appreciation for the imperfect dishes they serve. Lauren's mum's giblets have become family lore not because they don't love her, but because they do; because they can laugh at her and with her as much as my brother and I love and laugh at our mum's business-like efficiency in the kitchen. 'I'll use dried' is Mum's riposte to a recipe's requirement for fresh dill; 'Won't white wine vinegar do?' she'll say, when it specifies sherry vinegar; 'Crikey, not bothering with *that*,' she'll scoff at its insistence on homemade harissa. Sometimes she cuts a corner too far, but; mostly, it is indeed good enough.

In fact, Mum's cooking wasn't just 'good enough' growing up, it was very good – and infinitely preferable to the pre-prepared foods which proliferated during the 80s and 90s. As more women chose to juggle having a job with having children, mass-manufactured food brands sought to profit off their guilt by exploiting the idea that food = love. 'One of the 20th century's best known TV jingles ran "Nothing says lovin' like something from the oven" and came from Pilsbury, which made cake pre-mixes,' observes Kaori O'Connor, anthropologist and food historian. 'That idea that food is love was grafted onto the emergence of pre-made food and became part of that growing culture of performative parenting; of using novelty food and toys to say, "Look how much I love my child".'

She cites party bags as an example of this 'performative parenting' – which is funny to me because my parents were vehement party bag refuseniks. Where friends' mums would fill bright plastic bags with sweets, birthday cake, party poppers and even bath toys at the end of their parties, our parents doled out a satsuma and a (small) slice of cake. I'm not saying this made them better parents. Their refusal to conform to the excesses of kid-based consumerism reflected their puritanical natures more than their parenting skills, and it was only when the environmental impacts of single-use plastics materialised years later that we retrospectively forgave them. Besides, were my mother entirely immune to the pull of performative parenting, she wouldn't have spent so long on our cakes.

These cakes were extraordinary: high concept, elaborately constructed and themed either to us or the type of party we were having. There was a piano, a rat, a fairy castle, a farmyard – even, one year, a rocket, perched upright on its launchpad. Every birthday Nicholas and I would spend as much time perusing Jane Asher's book of party cakes as we did the Argos catalogue, greedily flicking through the sticky pages in search of that year's choice. I've said our mum sometimes cut corners whilst cooking; she didn't on these masterpieces. In part because we looked forward to them more than any other part of the party, in part because she likes baking. I suspect, it was also to prove to herself and everyone that yes, she worked full-time – but it didn't preclude baking her kids a birthday cake.

Sometimes she enjoyed it; often she felt the pressure, as I found out during the year of the rocket cake, hours before my brother's party. Walking into the garage to fetch a tennis ball, I discovered my mother elbow-deep in icing, fighting gravity as she tried to erect a long, vertical sponge on its narrowest point. The air was blue with curses, abandoned cake-covered triangles of cardboard abounded, and for the first time I sensed she wasn't quite as enamoured by the Jane Asher experience as we were. Though her efforts to meet our cake expectations were invariably very successful, I realise now they came at an emotional price.

Which brings us neatly to Nigella, Mum's counterpoint Delia, and the importance of both these women to women like my mother. Where Jane Asher offered fairy castles, and shop-bought cakes offered freedom from the kitchen, Delia and Nigella carved out the middle ground. They weren't scared of shortcuts – indeed they celebrated them, with Nigella famously passing off shop-bought hummus as her own and Delia eventually writing a book entitled *How to Cheat at Cooking*. At the same time, they knew that there were merits in cooking and baking which went beyond servicing others' needs, and toward forging relationships with a woman's loved ones and – heaven forbid – herself.

I remember my mum bringing home a copy of Nigella's *How to be a Domestic Goddess* and being struck by the sight of her in her sharp suit, leafing through a book with a cupcake on it. Only in adulthood have I come to appreciate the deep-seated feminism of Nigella, whose intellectual appeal to women is often lost in the froth around her more obvious appeal to men. In the book's introduction, Nigella swiftly and deftly puts paid to the notion that its title is anything other than ironic: 'What I'm talking about is not being a domestic goddess exactly, but feeling like one,' she writes.

Nigella created a kitchen in which brains, business and busy-ness were wholly compatible with cooking for pleasure. Her cakes looked impressive but were easy to execute. Mistakes were to be laughed at and covered with icing. That isn't to say she lowered standards, but that she never let the quest for perfection supersede that for comfort and love. Delia's recipes were – obviously – different, but in her legendary efficacy, she too showed women how to cook without compromising their independence. Her recipes work, the unofficial tagline ran, and in doing so they were empowering, allowing people to feed their families without faffing or stressing or feeling stupid because they've never heard of half the ingredients. With Delia or Nigella in hand, parents and children could simply enjoy each other's company, which could be one reason why Jane Asher's cake-shaped flights of fancy were gradually phased out in favour of Nigella's chocolate Malteser sponge.

My relationship with my mum through food has not been easy. Our false breastfeeding start proved auspicious, for no sooner had I outgrown the fairy castle cakes than I was developing the same anxieties around food and weight that had afflicted my mother in her younger years. As the pain she felt whilst breastfeeding me had become my pain, so the disordered approach to eating she had adopted throughout her twenties and thirties became mine as I attempted to whittle away my whippet-like body. My 'second dinner' of fruit, yoghurt and cereal became just fruit, then ceased entirely. The packed lunches she made were binned in favour of hitting the school gym. Where I could get away with not eating, I didn't eat; and where I couldn't, I mirrored her exactly, to the point where I would panic if I wasn't sitting near enough to her at mealtimes. From 14 right up until I left for university, every mouthful my mum took became my own.

When I started seeing a therapist in my mid-20s, she observed that my fixation with eating and weighing exactly what my mum ate and weighed had created a second and wildly distorted umbilical cord, a cord only I would be able to sever. That process took years – yet for all the physical and emotional fall out, it has strengthened our relationship immeasurably. The most striking example of this came about a month after I finished the first draft of this book, when Mum and I cycled the length of France. For 15 days, we ate, drank and pedalled the Vélodyssée, from Roscoff to Biarritz, via patisseries, farmers markets, oyster beds, fromageries, bars, cafés and crêperies. It was gastronomically glorious. It was also liberating for two people who have both struggled with their relationship with food to be forced to consider it as fuel, first and foremost. Quickly (and necessarily, for we were cycling around 50 miles a day) we settled into a delicious routine of breakfast, mid-morning pastry, lunch, afternoon cake, an aperitif, and the evening meal.

As we rode as equals so we ate as equals, navigating the menus just as we did the maps: together. One particularly hot, hard day we arrived in the canal-side town of Marans and decided to swap our slice of afternoon cake for two bowls of ice cream. It is hard to articulate just how fantastic saying 'Fuck it – we're having three scoops each' feels to two people used to denying themselves, but we were united in our decision to shake off those glace shackles. We traded spoonfuls with each other, of course, but we chose for ourselves and according to what we wanted, not what we deemed low fat. Suffice to say, I don't need the photo I took of my rapidly melting marron, vanilla and pistachio triple to recall the joy with which we seized our spoons in our dusty, sweaty hands and dove in.

In general, I steer well clear of the 'food is fuel' line of thought, finding it reductive at best and unhelpful at worst – but this felt different. Cycling through France, a country in which protein bars are a sin and the 'food is fuel' idea an abomination, we felt it more as a framework than a command. The daily act of donning our jerseys, charting our course over croissants, and pedalling from pitstop to pitstop created a rhythm which connected us to each other, as much as it did our bodies and bikes; a rhythm which rendered us equals. Mum and I had already redefined our relationship to each other through food, but those fifteen days fortified it through the sheer force of momentum. Side by side, revolution by revolution, we consolidated what we both knew: that we were best friends, as well as being mother and child.

Indeed, if there is one upshot to our both having had such tortured relationships with food, it is the insight it has given me into how challenging it can be to feed your kids, for all that society presents it as natural. Those quick, cobbled-together teas our mums make – the Friday night risottos, cheesy pastas, cheese on toasts – straddle this tension between a child's 'simple' demands and the complexities of their mother's own life, and dish up a happy medium: a meal that leaves everyone feeling loved and relaxed.

In France, roadside lunches of hand-torn baguette stuffed with fresh tomatoes and local cheese became our grown-up equivalent of that cheesy pasta: an easy meal we enjoyed all the more for its simplicity. This was the food we had dreamed of during lockdown, longing for the day when we might freewheel along French lanes, baguettes sticking out of our panniers like flags. Like easy teas, these lunches were fuel, born largely of necessity – but they were laced with an almost giddy contentment. There was no pressure on Mum to prepare it, or on me to enjoy it; no choice as to whether or not we ate it. Indeed, there was nothing to do but chew, chat and get back on our bikes.

Recipe: Mum's cheesy pasta

Thinking about this dish – and better still, eating this dish – I understand why Italian nonnas feel so strongly about their pasta recipes, even if they would balk at this one. Every aspect matters: the shells that clasp the bright, beady vegetables, the sharp salty tang of the Tickler cheese, the sweet kick of the wholegrain mustard cutting through the creamy sauce. Please don't deviate – or if you do, don't invite me round to try it. Make a bit too much and serve in deep pasta bowls.

Ingredients, for four
25g/¾oz butter
25g/¾oz plain flour
300ml/10½fl oz milk
2 tbsp wholegrain mustard
200g /7oz Tickler extra mature Cheddar, grated (plus more to sprinkle top)
400g/14oz conchiglie (pasta shells)
50g /2oz frozen sweetcorn
50g /2oz frozen peas
Salt and pepper

Method
Melt the butter in a saucepan on a medium heat then stir in the flour. Cook for one minute, then gradually add the milk, stirring well between each addition. Bring to the boil, stirring, then simmer for 2 minutes, before stirring in the mustard, almost all the cheese and the seasoning.

Meanwhile, cook the pasta, adding the sweetcorn and peas for the final two minutes. Heat the bowls in the oven or microwave. Drain the pasta and vegetables, then return to the pan and pour in the cheesy sauce. Stir and serve with the remaining cheese scattered on top.

4

Angela's Chicken Soup

Feeders and feelings

'Can I get you something to eat,' Angela says by way of greeting, her expression a familiar blend of concern and brisk practicality. In the background my best friend – her daughter, Sophie – hovers, hoping that for once her mum will win me over but knowing, as ever that she won't. I decline, as I always do, even whilst my growling stomach begs to the contrary. Angela insists, as she always does, bargaining scrambled eggs on toast down to just toast, down to half a slice, down to a satsuma. Angela is a feeder and proud of it, and there are few things more confounding to a feeder than an eating disorder, a disease where eating is both the condition and the cure.

Today Angela and I can laugh about it: her persistence, my resistance, her baffled disappointment at food manifestly failing to do what she had always believed it would do: solve problems. 'My brain says it doesn't, always, but my heart says it does. It's the way I am wired. I'm a stereotypical feeder,' she tells me decades later, over a tea and a banana muffin she's insisted on buying me one cold January afternoon. In a long history of her showing her love for people through feeding them, I was a rare exception – though as I point out, the love which fuelled her offers of food was never lost on me. On the contrary, the guilt I felt when I could not accept and show my appreciation weighed on me with every plate I rejected. When feeding is so bound up with feeling, not eating is as difficult for the would-be diner as it is for the would-be cook.

For Angela, born and raised in a family where her grand-mother cooked as constantly as breathing, food has always been the glue that binds people together. 'Day in, day out, we cook – and we reinforce those bonds by cooking,' she enthuses. Even her animals – a dog, a cat and a couple of local foxes, all of whom she prepares homecooked meals for – aren't immune to her need to feed. Where some people connect with themselves and others through clubs, crafts or classes, Angela connects through food, regularly asking her now-adult children what they're having for dinner and lunch now she cannot always feed them. Where my mum and grandma cook for a host of reasons, of which love is just one, Angela's cooking has a religious quality to it. 'It is first and last an expression of love, for me.'

This religious quality is not just pseudo, but literal. Angela is Ashkenazi Jewish. The feeding Jewish mum is a cultural cliché, but like all clichés it has some roots in reality. 'When your people have been persecuted historically, you know the pleasures and significance of a good meal; of being able to provide a good meal to your family,' she explains. Mealtimes are embedded in Jewish family life because they know time is precious, and time with loved ones is most precious of all. It's a philosophy which, post my parents' divorce, I could relate to on a minor level: I was obsessed with our family eating *together*. I would start rounding my brothers and parents up at least ten minutes prior to dinner or pre-dinner-drinks time. Even now, this herding instinct is a familial tick. I am not Jewish and will never, ever begin to understand the cumulative cultural anxiety born of historical oppression; but I can see how eating with your family every Friday without fail feels like a means of imposing order on a world that feels – and often was, for Jewish people – chaotic and terrifying.

My family reckon this impulse and my general obsession with food makes *me* a feeder – and perhaps I am, to a certain extent. I'll admit to strongarming friends into second portions and springing treats on everyone, even if they really don't want treats. Doubtless being a feeder, like any psychological quirk, exists on the spectrum on which we all sit, somewhere between pure eaters and pure feeders. Yet there is an honesty and simplicity to Angela's feeding which is echoed in the mums and grandmas of other friends, and which I do not necessarily see in me.

When I was anorexic, I cooked to cover my tracks. I cooked because I wanted to eat, couldn't eat, and so projected my appetite onto loved ones. Since being in recovery, I have cooked and hosted in part to redefine myself as someone who eats, as well as feeds. How I see myself, how I want to be seen, and how I can shape myself (literally), and my relationship with others all dictate how and what I feed people. 'Why are you baking those?' Melanie demanded once, when I was busying myself with a batch of chocolate brownies as a teenager. 'You're not going to eat any of them. You're making them to make *us* eat brownies.' I wasn't being wholly selfish – I wasn't looking to do a Hansel and Gretel on my family – but she was right that my motives had a lot to do with my own frustrated needs.

Compare this to Angela's grandmother, who would never sit down at dinner – never even take her apron off, lest she be required to rustle up more food. Compare it to all of the nonnas, yayas and nonyas whose homes you simply can't enter without submitting to a substantial meal. In 2019, British-Greek journalist and author Anastasia Miari set out to gather recipes and stories from grandmothers across the world, which she eventually compiled in a book called *Grand Dishes*. She found their generosity was overwhelming, particularly in southern and eastern Europe and Asia. 'You'd arrive looking to ask about and sample one recipe – and find they'd prepared five enormous courses,' she laughs. 'Particularly in Italy, Greece, Georgia and Azerbaijan, there was this constant rolling out of the red carpet for us, through the universal love language of food.'

Anastasia cannot account for this variation across countries – though she stresses that all the grandmas were generous, with time and life advice if not a huge dinner. She suspects the difference is cultural: 'In Greece for example we have a concept called *theoxenia*, which loosely translated means "kindness to foreigners". It dates back to the Ancient Greek period when people believed Zeus would strike you if you didn't show kindness to people you didn't know. That has been preserved over the centuries no matter what social and political changes [occurred], and it's definitely rubbed off on me,' she laughs. 'You cannot possibly come to my house and not have something to drink, and some feta and olives.' Yet whilst Anastasia, like me, sees that impulse to host and feed as part of her identity, she didn't think the same could be said of the grandmothers she spoke to. 'I'd ask them if they felt it was important to cook, and they'd look baffled and say, "Well, of course. It's like breathing. It's just what you do each day to live".'

For these women raising a family in the mid-20th century, there wasn't the option to eat out, buy in or have a career outside the kitchen. In affectionately characterising these women as 'feeders' – and I do with my grandma all the time – it's easy to forget that for much of their lives, feeding was more a chore than a choice. My grandma cooked because she had children to feed, then because she had a hotel to feed, then because there were grandchildren, including ourselves and our cousins, whose parents also worked full-time and who she cooked almost daily meals for. Whether she enjoyed it was not a question that crossed our minds, or indeed her mind. 'I don't really think about it,' she told me when I asked her. She became a feeder – our feeder – by default.

This is not to detract from the pleasure her meals brought to us, and to her via our visible, audible enjoyment. She loved and still loves the way her cooking unites us physically when we're gathered around her table, and conversationally when we're apart. Her casseroles and cakes are our lingua franca: foods we know and love, which transcend our differences and distances. My cousin and I can and do quibble over the royal family, politics and the relative merits of veganism – but can reminisce happily about Grandma's steak and kidney pie or her ground rice cake, slathered in butter: dishes that are a familial touchstone even though we seldom eat them now.

Again, there is a religious quality to all of these dishes and the way we speak of them, something totemic. Even when my brother and I were eating Grandma's meals after school, decanting them from Stork and Carte D'Or tubs out of the freezer, they felt greater than the sum of their parts. In her absence and, until she came home, the absence of our mum, Grandma's rich, buttery shepherd's pie felt like a talisman. We ate it with Henderson's Relish, which my grandad mail-ordered from his hometown of Sheffield even after the advent of the Internet, and we felt connected to them both. Today, Grandma's old habit of pressing food upon us when we visit shows no sign of dying: even if we've cycled or trained there, she'll insist upon slipping us something. 'Travel safely. Precious cargo,' she'll smile, slipping a tenner and a foil-wrapped slice of cake into our pockets or panniers as we depart.

My friend and fellow food writer Gurdeep Loyal attributes the pseudo-religious nature of feeders' feeding to their being mostly matriarchs: mums and grandmas in charge of the household. They hold sway over a matriarchal culture in which 'the kitchen is like their temple. You enter, and there is an exchange, but ultimately they hold court there,' he muses over cocktails in a London bar that feels a far cry from the warm fug of our respective matriarchs' realms. Gurdeep was born in Leicester to Punjabi Indian parents and confirms what several Punjabi friends have observed, which is that when it comes to feeding, 'there is a sense you should always have an appetite, no matter how you are feeling.' He continues, 'If you're happy, you should eat to show happiness. If you're unhappy you should eat as a remedy.' What you cannot do is *not* eat. Eating is an act of submission to their cooking and, by extension, to their love.

'This display of feeding says, I'm going to give you more than you will ever want or need, and you will never be able to bottom it. It says, you will never tire of my love, and I will never tire of loving you,' says Gurdeep. It is that largesse which feels religious, even when the feeder is no longer a person of faith. Like me, Gurd grew up in a multicultural urban area, where Jewish and Indian families rubbed shoulders. 'My best friend Daniel was Jewish, and our mums really got on. They were constantly swapping dishes,' he recalls. 'We spent so much time going between each other's houses, eating really good Jewish food and Punjabi food, we were both really fat as children. We still joke about being Tweedledee and Tweedledum.'

He can laugh about it now, but Gurdeep's recollections point toward the dark underbelly of complications that can come with growing up with a feeder. When Gurd left home for university he lost a lot of weight very quickly, discovering a shape and persona that existed outside of his food-centric familial identity. Being slim meant he could fit into 'cooler' clothes, date 'cooler' people – and as a result, he came to associate being fat with his culture. In his second or third year of university he stopped eating Indian food entirely. 'I felt that my culture was the reason I was a fat child,' he recalls, 'when of course it wasn't my culture, really. It was me.'

For his mother and aunties, this rejection felt personal. 'It came across like a rejection of them and their love,' he remembers. We tend to think of the feeder as more concerned with those they feed than they are with their own feelings and requirements, but Gurdeep argues the reverse is often true. 'Their response to us not eating or, more telling still, their *not* feeding for once, is often a clearer sign of their own emotions than it is of ours' he observes, which is why occasionally, being plied with food can feel less like love, more like edible blackmail. I've lost count of the times my brother has gone to bed with stomach ache because he's felt obliged to polish off every last morsel Grandma's cooked in order to please her. By the same token, when Grandma declares she can't be bothered to bake a cake or a pudding for when so-and-so comes round, what she really means is she's angry, unhappy or unwell.

My own response to Grandma's feeding tendencies was more complicated still – or at least, it was when I hit my teenage years and became consumed by eating disorders. My transformation into a fastidious, rake-thin teen was sudden and surprising, given the guileless simplicity with which I'd gobbled up Grandma's food as a child. If my cousins were around, we'd have eating contests, piling squat, squishy Yorkshires onto our plates, and shovelling them down with gravy quickly so we could head back out to the garden. Come dessert I would eagerly accept second, third and fourth helpings of pudding, using a spatula to eke the last of the custard onto my warm, wobbling sponge doused in golden treacle. In fact, such was my Bird's custard habit my grandad continued to call me custard face long after my sweet tooth had ceased.

Like Angela, my grandparents were by turns saddened and baffled by my eating disorders, which continued to grow throughout my teens and early twenties. My mother had an eating disorder in her teens and twenties, so she was familiar with the tell-tale signs. She knew the tricks, like filling up with water or suddenly turning vegetarian. She knew the metrics, like 'just one roast potato' or 'a slither' of pudding. She knew the excuses for not eating – 'I've got a big dinner later' or 'I had a big breakfast' – and she knew precisely what I was doing when after an unusually large portion of pudding, I headed swiftly upstairs.

My body still recoils in shame at the memory of Grandad's knock at the bathroom door, and his face when he entered; at the soft anger in his voice and the uncomprehending pain in his eyes when he confirmed what he feared. Quite what he said to me then is lost in a haze of humiliation, all I know is that I've never felt the connection between food and love more keenly. To purge shop-bought puddings was bad enough, to purge my grandma's blackcurrant pie and my beloved Bird's custard was blasphemy. If Gurdeep's theory is right and a feeder's kitchen is their temple, there could have been no greater sin.

Even now I wish I'd said no to the pie. As pained as Grandma would have been, she'd have far rather that rejection than the one I subsequently inflicted. I know refusing food makes one feel on the fringes of a feeder's love, but bulimia plunges you into a perfect storm. I loved blackcurrant pie and custard. Most of all, I loved Grandma, whose eyes light up when you ask for seconds, and who rewards you with the best bits like the caramelised crusts and runaway fruit, bleeding their juices into the pastry. But submitting to that love through food awakened an opposite, but no less fierce desire for autonomy and vicious control.

It was a terrible bind. I ate to love and feel loved, to be the easy eater I once was – then in panic, rejected it. I ate to feel connected, purged to feel in control and as a result I felt nothing at all. That's the funny thing about emotional eating, or at least that kind of emotional eating: you never really *taste* anything, so you eat more and more in search of feeling and flavour. At my worst I contemplated my next mouthful whilst chewing, hoping against hope that *that* one would satisfy me; knowing, even as I swallowed, it could never fill the void.

It's a sensation I have since heard echoed by many who have suffered with bulimia or binge eating. 'You're never quite in the moment of pleasure,' reflects Bee Wilson. A former binge eater herself, Bee describes feeling at times like the Martin Amis character who famously starts to crave his next cigarette while smoking his first. Bulimia and binge eating disorders thrive in a vacuum, and on food that is cheap and anonymous: 'Pringles, Häagen Dazs, Crunchy Nut cornflakes – food which is highly processed and easy to binge on,' Bee observes. She remembers how it felt to be a child in the feeder's equivalent of Eden, 'before there were calories. Before there was good or bad food. I can remember as a child of six or seven running in from the cold, hungry and delighted and eating eggy bread until I was full or the plate was empty.' In substance and in spirit it's a far cry from the supermarket biscuits she recalls mindlessly binge eating in her later years.

There's nothing straightforward about feeders and feelings – either their own, or those of the people they're feeding. Yet for me, Bee and many others I've met, food made with that intensity of love has been the best defence against disordered eating, and the best road to recovery afterwards. I'd be lying if I said Grandad's knock on the bathroom door was my Damascene moment. My eating issues prevailed for many more years – but after his intervention, I could no longer deny the link between my grandmother's love and her cooking; between her urge to protect me, and her butter-slathered ground rice cake. I still struggled elsewhere, but I could no longer purge her food which, like a force field, kept my illness at bay for as long as I was under her care.

Recipe: Angela's Chicken Soup

The soup she 'could make whilst standing on [her] head', Angela has been cooking this recipe almost every week since childhood. It remains one of her favourite dishes, and it's one of Sophie's too; her cheesy pasta equivalent, her hug in a bowl. Angela serves it with matzo balls, and when telling me this, reminds me of Marilyn Monroe's famous retort to her Jewish husband Arthur Miller, when he first offered them to her: 'So what did they do with the rest of the matzo?' She also suggests ringing the changes every so often, by adding a parsnip and parsley for a slightly sweeter soup. As for the imprecision around quantities, Angela tells me Jews are rubbish at precise measurements – or at least this one is!

Ingredients, for four
8 chicken thighs, skins removed
4 or 5 large carrots, cut into discs
3 or 4 celery stalks, cut into chunks
2 large onions, cut into wedges
A large fistful of vermicelli
Matzo balls
Salt and pepper

Method
Bring to the boil all ingredients except the vermicelli and matzo balls, then simmer gently for about 1–1¼ hours.

Taste for seasoning. Before serving, cook the vermicelli, then drain and put into bowls before ladling soup on top. Finish by topping with matzo balls, if required.

5

Jayshree's Gulab Jamun

Sweet love

Though millionaire's shortbread was and is my favourite thing that Grandma makes, ground rice cake is what we love most as a family. There is no recipe for ground rice cake; not one that resembles my grandma's, and hers is in her head or – perhaps more accurately – in her hands and eyes. It's nothing to look at: dense, plain and pale, with none of the burnished gold or fluffy rise of more familiar sponges. Yet when thickly sliced and slathered with butter, it is unbeatable – and all the better for being 'ours'.

Grandma's ground rice cake speaks to a principle that pastry chef Ravneet Gill touches on in her beautiful, technicoloured baking book, *Sugar, I Love You*. Contrary to its title, Ravneet's book is not simply a love letter to sugar. Indeed, many of its recipes don't even contain much sugar. 'We all love to indulge in sweet things, but moderation is what makes me love sugar,' she writes in her introduction. 'Only when sugar is truly understood and used to balance pastry and desserts does it really shine.'

Ground rice cake doesn't contain much sugar, either. It is sweet, but it is also milky, savoury – even a bit salty. We enjoy its sweetness, of course, but only as part of the sliced, buttered whole. What I love about Ravneet's observation is that it encapsulates how baking can be not just an act of love, but a metaphor for it; for those relationships which are built not just on sweet words, but on quality time and authenticity. Grandma doesn't dish out affection or praise like sweets. She doesn't dish out sweets at all, come to think of it. But when she does, it tastes all the sweeter for being both measured and heartfelt – like the sugar in ground rice cake.

That's true of my grandma, at least; and yet, in the wider world, our relationships to and through sugar are neither so pure nor so simple. Though cheap and commonplace now, sugar's historic status as a precious commodity lives on in its use as a shorthand for congratulations, commiserations and love. Feeling sorry for yourself? Have some chocolate. Feeling sorry for a friend? Give them some chocolate. Ditto feeling happy, concerned, appreciative, contrite or proud. Of course, this devotion to sugar has generated some of society's most devastating problems, from slavery to obesity; yet out of it has been born the glittering world of confectionary and all our associated memories. We might lament the soaring rates of type 2 diabetes and the children going to school on a coke and a Twix bar, but how many parents would deprive their kids the chance to blow out the candles on their birthday cake, hunt chocolate eggs in the garden come Easter or during Diwali, devour gajar ka halwa and barfi?

Look around and, for better or worse, the shimmering seam of sugar runs through almost all human relations. At its most obvious, it is the currency with which we win over our children, using its deprivation as punishment and its gift as reward. I virtuously wrote that Grandma didn't dish out sweets – but she did give us money with the express instruction to spend it on pick 'n' mix if we were going to Brighton for the day (and to buy her some liquorice whilst we were at it), and she did use sherbets as bait if we had a long walk ahead of us. In doing so, she too became part of a long tradition of grandparents using sweet treats to bond with their grandchildren – sometimes to the despair of their often more health-conscious parents.

Growing up on the Greek island of Corfu, Anastasia Miari recalls how her Corfiot pappou used to buy her ice cream every day on the way back from school and, if he was walking her there, a chocolate croissant. Her English mother would have despaired if she'd known – but for Anastasia and her grandpa their ice cream ritual crystallised their close bond. 'It was soothing and joyful. Whenever I was upset, I would run to pappou and he would take me for ice cream,' she recalls, laughing. It delighted her, and it pleased him to be the person she ran to; the one who could, for just a few drachma, ease her childish pain with this sweet and deliciously mischievous balm.

Looking back as an adult, Anastasia can see the selfishness of that need to feel on side with a child, contrary to their health and the wishes of their mother or father. As Bee observed of her estranged dad, sending her off on the train back to her mum's with a large box of Maltesers, 'to give a child the things she loves to eat bestows a heroic glow'. Bee's dad agonised about the divorce and the effect on his children, one of whom was lurching toward anorexia, the other of whom – Bee – was heading in the opposite direction, equally unhappily. Only when she became a parent herself did she realise that the person her father was rewarding 'was primarily himself'.

In conclusion, Bee wrote, in what would become one of her most widely quoted sentences, 'sugar is not love. But it can feel like it'. Even when the medium by which that sugar arrives is objectively quite bad – like, say, Angel Delight – it can feel synonymous with comfort and warmth. Writing this, I can already hear the outraged cries of my fellow millennials, shocked that I could cast a shadow over this bubbly, sweet token of our collective childhoods – and I hear you, friends. I too enjoyed many a strawberry or banana Angel Delight at Mum's or my friend Amy's, where her mum would grandly serve it in wine glasses. But we should remember that it was not just the flavour of the powdery cocktail of palm oil, starch, emulsifiers, gelling agents, anti-caking agents, colours, flavourings and sugar which was sparking joy.

It was the context: like the wine glasses Amy and I would monitor like sentinels, unable to resist opening the fridge door every two minutes to check on their progress. Invariably we'd lose patience and slurp the Delight down underset and wobbly, which is why Amy's mum dished them out in a glass. My mum exacted more patience – partly because she too loved Angel Delight so would insist on bringing us our bowls herself with one or two telling spoonfuls missing. It wasn't a common ritual, but it was one we only had at her house and given Mum's health-consciousness at all other times, there was a delicious complicity to it. Even now I can conjure up the sweet sense of anticipation that accompanied the sound of her whisking the magical powder into the milk with a fork and instructing us to wait half an hour.

Taken at face value there's nothing wrong with this nostalgia for a dessert which forged such strong connections between my mum, brother and I, and between me and Amy. Indeed, such is the universality of Angel Delight that simply asking someone roughly my age what their favourite flavour was is bound to spark an animated discussion: when I message friends asking their thoughts on Angel Delight, my phone pings non-stop with stories of sibling rivalry, favoured toppings and designated Angel Delight spoons and bowls – showing that, at their best, these mass-manufactured childhood treats serve as a portal both to other people and to the people we once were.

At their worst – and the two often come hand in hand – they become compulsive: something we turn to as adults in distress in the hope they can deliver the same comfort they did when we were children. They rarely do. On the contrary, as adults we are more likely to be dissatisfied with these cocktails of sugar and chemicals, and we are better able – when they fail to fill that emotional void – to buy and eat more. What we seek in the bottom of a tub of Ben and Jerry's is not so much flavour as feeling, or the memory of a feeling bound up with cookie-dough studded ice cream or the scrapings of a cake bowl. The design of our olfactory system and the way we process flavours in the brain's prefrontal context – the area also responsible for remembering – means that flavour and memory are so aligned as to be almost synonymous. This is true of all flavours, not just sweet ones; yet it is sweetness that, thanks to the chemical high it induces, has become the most deftly woven into our childhood memories of affection, celebration, consolation, and reward.

This is not always a terrible thing. In the right place, time and quantity there is a lot to love about sugar. As I touched on in the last chapter, there is a long-standing and large difference between mass-manufactured treats and homemade ones, both in how they're made and – by extension – how they're consumed. At school our classmate Khushboo would bring in a Tupperware of sweets every Diwali: halwa, jalebi and my favourite, mohanthal, a fudgy square studded with nuts and flavoured with saffron. I took them for granted as a child, but I learnt many years later that it takes women in Hindu and Sikh families several days and many hands to make all these confectionary jewels.

Over batata pawa my friend Vivek's mum Jayshree tells me how, during one of the Covid lockdowns, her daughter announced a craving for gulab jamun, an Indian sweet that takes hours to prepare and cook. 'I told her, if I'm making it, you're making it with me,' she laughs. 'You have to make the dough, rest it, knead it – really knead it – then roll it out, shape and fry it.' She shows me a photo. The sweet is beautiful: a delicate and doubtless delectable tribute to their culinary heritage, craftsmanship and the time they spent together during the pandemic. 'You can buy these ready-made,' Jayshree comments, flicking through more shots, 'but my children refuse to eat them. They aren't the same.'

I am reminded of my grandma's millionaire's shortbread, the mass-produced equivalent of which can be found in shops and cafés around the country. Often, they are too sweet andinevitably they fail to hit the spot, being devoid of those intangible but essential ingredients like love, tradition and time. Sugar isn't bad, per se – but it has become devalued, says

Shuk Ng, a pastry chef and friend through Borough Market where she works part-time at my favourite greengrocers Ted's Veg. 'Artisan bakers, pastry chefs – our grandparents, even – spend so long learning to do what they do, but when people can buy the same thing in Tesco they don't understand the work that's gone into it, or the quality of the ingredients. It gives you the enjoyment of sugar, but nothing else around it,' she observes.

By being ubiquitous, these cakes are rendered anonymous. What little personality they have comes from their packaging, which plays upon our real or perceived memories of when they *were* homemade, or a treat from the local bakery. Again, it comes back to moderation, a subject on which Rav and Shuk are in alignment. 'I think when you're eating things made with too much sugar or sweetener then what you enjoy and crave more of is just sweetness,' says Shuk. 'I moderate how much sugar I have and use, because sugar is something I always want to be able to appreciate.' On a bad day – one of the few times she really craves chocolate – she will sooth herself with a square of high-quality chocolate and enjoy the whole experience: the snap, the smooth texture, the way it lingers and melts in her mouth. Done well, pastries, cakes and desserts are designed to be enjoyed slowly: for their small but perfect forms to be deconstructed and deliberated over, for their component parts by turns admired and savoured.

At their best, these sweet treats feel like a communion between creator and eater. Shuk recalls how, when she worked in The Ivy, she would cheer when an order came through for a dish she particularly favoured; for when someone eats and enjoys something she has made, in a way that shows appreciation for the care she's put into it, it feels like more has been exchanged than simply dessert. There is a considered way of eating that satisfies all parties, whether it's my grandma making shortbread in the kitchen for her family, or Shuk making intricate patisserie for her celebrity diners. It is, observes Bee, the culinary equivalent of using your phone to chat to a loved one instead of mindlessly scrolling through Instagram and 'liking' their endeavours.

'There are nourishing ways of interacting with phones, and there are junk food ways of interreacting with them,' Bee continues. 'The same is true of sugar.' On one end of the spectrum, you have a guest savouring and sharing their birthday chocolate bomb with friends at The Ivy; on the other, my friend Lauren, who once described binge eating Magnums and, like that Martin Amis character, thinking about the crack and slurp of the second before she'd finished the first. We live in a world in which food *is* emotional; not inherently so, but rendered thus by ritual, identity, marketing and consumerism. 'Sugar is sugar,' says Bee. 'If you allow sugar to be sugar, then you can have a healthy relationship with it – but if you are trying to make sugar *love* then I don't see how you can.'

Yet where does love start, and sugar end? How do we extricate two things which feel and can even sometimes look inextricable? After all, the idea that food is love was seized upon by food brands from the Second World War onwards, as the rapid expansion of processed foods coincided with the rise of more permissive and performative styles of parenting. 'The entire war effort was switched to commercial production – and a lot of that was focused on food and toys for children. Parental love was far more openly expressed, and children could be spoiled in a way their parents couldn't be previously,' explains anthropologist Kaori

O'Connor. Once sugar rationing was over, that spoiling could – and increasingly did – include ice cream, sweets and chocolate. This was the heyday of big, universally consumed ad campaigns; of slogans and commercials, catchy jingles and mascots. What pre-made food lacked in the way of ritual and tradition, these campaigns provided in the way of Tony the Tiger, having a KitKat on a coffee break, and collectable toys and cards.

Millennials and their parents may recall the 'last Rolo' campaign, launched in 1980 in the run up to Valentine's Day and repeated annually for 20 years hence. The result was that, every February, Nestlé's memorable strapline – 'Do you love anyone enough to give them your last Rolo?' – resounded around schools and offices. At my school you could even send a solo Rolo, wrapped in cheap purple fabric with an anonymous note, to your crush in the nearby boy's school. The boys could send a Rolo too, but they rarely did unless instructed to by their girlfriends. Come Valentine's Day these would be unwrapped with giggling ceremony, to the palpable envy of the rest of us as we feigned an indifference we didn't really feel.

I'm over it; really, I am – but it is a compelling example of how food brands can weave themselves into our emotional lives. Often this is the result of clever marketing colluding with hazy childhood memories. Sometimes, like the Rolo's campaign, it is more explicit. In 2002 Magnum launched a collection of ice creams named and flavoured for the seven deadly sins: lust, sloth, greed, gluttony, envy, vanity and revenge. I was delighted, until it came to choosing my flavour – at which point I was plunged into something of an existential crisis. I knew what flavour I favoured – peanut butter ice cream with white chocolate – but I didn't relate to sloth, the sin it symbolised. I could have had it anyway, but I felt like doing so would redefine me as someone who was slothful, even though the sin I related to most at the time was envy.

I was being ridiculous, of course. Most people I've spoken to since say they went for the flavour they wanted, not the sin that most spoke to them. Yet branded food often speaks to identity and this is why it becomes so tangled up with love, because we feel instinctively drawn to the people who also prefer Hobnobs to Digestive biscuits or who eat their Creme Eggs the same way. Magnum tapped into that impulse. When the seven deadly sins collection launched, an executive close to the campaign told press they would counter the idea that 'good girls only eat lettuce and go to the gym' with the message that indulgence is 'acceptable' for women – 'empowering', even. That they could be so blatantly patronising seems extraordinary now, but the fact remains that – so long as you are as slim and beautiful as the women in the adverts – eating a Magnum feels like self-love; a moment in which you eat a chocolate-covered ice cream and inhabit your 'sin'.

It is easy to point the finger at food brands. They are the ones capitalising on our relationship with sugar, and to other people through sugar. They, or at least the forces that enabled their existence, are the ones who made sugar cheap and accessible, transforming it from a prized luxury to everyday treat. There are myriad socioeconomic factors fuelling the obesity epidemic – but if we're naming names, it is Nestlé and Mars, not Shuk and Jayshree with their homemade, hand-rolled pastries. Yet Pandora's chocolate box has been opened, and even if we were able to, I'm not sure any of us would want to close the lid.

Even the most industrious baker, the most abstemious eschewer of shop-bought sweets, will be able to point to a branded biscuit or chocolate that means something to them; that connects them to their loved ones. Jayshree's gulab jamun are special, but so too is the bowl of Lindors by the front door, for guests (and her kids) to take as they leave. I love Grandma's ground rice cake, but the smell of ginger snaps is almost as sacred, being reminiscent of her and my grandad's ritual of having one with a cup of tea in bed every morning. I remember the rare occasions at their hotel when the grandchildren were allowed to join them: snuggling under the covers and learning from Grandad how to dunk the biscuit *just* long enough to take the edge off the snap without it sinking.

Grandma rarely buys them for herself now, but when she does, I can't resist lifting the lid of the biscuit tin and breathing in. The last present I bought my grandad before he died was ginger biscuits from Fortnum and Mason's. He loved them, he told me, but they weren't quite the same as McVitie's – 'and they're only 99p in Lidl, Clare!' he said, excitedly.

Again, it comes back to Rav's point about moderation, about loving sugar for the sweetness it brings to the situation, not in its own right. Like the CLUB biscuits my brother and I used to have with Mum each morning, none of these moments would have been bettered by having another CLUB, a second ginger snap or a couple more Lindor balls. On the contrary, these snacks derive much of their significance from *being* limited, from our anticipating and savouring each sweet mouthful. One of the most heart-warming stories Bee tells me is of her grandparents who, whilst courting, would make an entire date out of sharing a simple two-fingered KitKat halfway through a walk.

Were they to have had a whole KitKat each, this story would not be worth telling; its power lies in their making so much out of something so small and, to our minds, quotidian. The anecdote shows how much our environment has changed since their time – for they weren't more virtuous than we are, says Bee. They just didn't have five varieties of KitKat chunky shouting from every shop counter. It also rather beautifully illustrates another way in which a healthy relationship with sugar and sweets can mirror a healthy relationship with someone we love, be it friend, lover or family: for the real hallmark of having had a really good time with another person is to be left wanting more.

Recipe: Jayshree's gulab jamun

Given I've never made gulab jamun and barely eaten it since school, I'm not best placed to comment on this one, nor to tinker with the methodology. Here then is Jayshree's recipe in its entirety, complete with smileys.

Ingredients, makes 100
½ cup warm milk
¾ cup coarse semolina
2 cups milk powder
½ tsp bicarbonate of soda
3 tbsp self-raising flour
1 tsp crushed cardamom
Sunflower oil, for frying

FOR THE SUGAR SYRUP

3 cups granulated sugar
3 cups water
Pinch of saffron

Method
Warm the milk and whisk in the semolina, then leave to rest for half an hour. In a large mixing bowl, add the milk powder, flour, cardamom and semolina mixture, and knead until smooth. Roll the dough into 2.5cm/1in balls.

Heat the oil for frying in a small pan up to a medium heat and fry the balls in batches until golden brown. Remove from the oil with a slotted spoon and leave to drain on kitchen paper.

Make the sugar syrup by adding all the ingredients to a saucepan, and boil until slightly thickened. The trick to get this right is to place a drop of syrup on a plate, then lift the plate, allowing the syrup to run. The syrup is ready when the liquid runs like a tear ☹.

Add the fried balls and the syrup to a flat-bottomed container. Cover, and let them sit overnight in the fridge. Cut one ball to make sure the syrup has soaked through.

Enjoy and eat! 😊

6

A 90s Packed Lunch

Forging friendships through food

'Do you remember your mint Viscounts?' my school friend Jenny asked once, during one of our long, wine-and-fajita-fuelled reminiscences. I laughed, struck by the memory. It was years since I'd thought of it, but I did suddenly recall peeling a Slytherin-green wrapper off a round mint-chocolate biscuit at lunch time and carefully smoothing it out. 'You cut the biscuit into three every time – three tiny pieces, so you could share them with me and Amy. One time you cut it into three pieces, and absent-mindedly ate all of them – and we shouted at you, like we were really annoyed.' She looked amused, if pained. 'You were so apologetic about it, I've always felt a bit guilty. I can't believe we let you share your tiny Viscount every day.'

It's a sweet, silly story, though I recognise much of myself in it: my eagerness to please, my readiness to apologise, my early neuroticism around food, friends and identity. I'd love to say my cutting an already small biscuit into three was born purely out of generosity, but it was more that I wanted to be liked. Amongst the packed lunch girls at school, food was status and currency, and my homemade wholegrain cheese sandwiches brought neither rank nor value. Next to the coolness conferred by Dairylea Dunkers, Cheesestrings and Müller Corners with chocolate cereal, the mint Viscount was all I had.

So I divvied it up, anxious to cement the friendships I had only forged since switching to packed lunches half way through junior school. Our school invariably divided along lunch lines and, though I'd known Jenny and Amy from kindergarten, it wasn't until I gave up on the school canteen that they went from classmates to friends. Until senior school those with packed lunches weren't even allowed to eat in the dining room, lest they tempt its paid-up members away with their cool Frubes and Tracker bars. We huddled in the unheated sports hall, laughing through our sandwiches at all the schmucks queuing up for their lunch, smug in the knowledge that we'd have first dibs on the stilts and the pogo sticks when we went out to play.

Back then, of course, the goal was to gulp lunch down and get into the playground, yet as we get older our moments with mates are almost entirely reduced to mealtimes, making school dinners something of a dress rehearsal for adulthood. Packed lunch with Jenny and Amy was my first taste of friendships forming around food rather than Brownies, ballet or parents chatting at the school gate. Every day we sat at the same table, in the same place, and pooled our crisp packets like pirates sharing the spoils; for, whilst our mums eschewed most of the trendy, new-fangled snack food of the 1990s, they did concede Skips, Chipsticks, Wotsits, Quavers, Space Raiders and – my favourite – pickled onion Monster Munch.

Though we weren't then au fait with the technique of splitting the crisp packet, our ritual was good practice for the pubs of our futures, when chucking a couple of packets onto the centre of the table and gesturing to people to help themselves is a staple of socialising. I remember the first crisp packet I split post pandemic; pulling carefully at the back seam, worried I'd lost the knack over lockdown. When it finally peeled apart into a shiny, silver sharing platter, its golden flakes fanning out so we could tuck in hungrily, we cheered. Though the times and places in which people might come together for food and drink are numerous and ever growing, there remains something totemic about this – despite or perhaps even because it is so basic. There's nothing dignified or hygienic about six different hands diving into one packet of ready salted, but you can't help but feel closer to people after fighting their salt-flecked fingers for the crunchiest, knobbliest shards.

As anthropologist Martin Jones observed in his 2008 book *Feast*, 'the sharing of food brings people once again to the intimate interconnection between social person and biological organism'. In other words, by splitting a packet of crisps, taking a few and gesturing to the rest of the table, we acknowledge our own humanness and that of everyone else. This might sound a grandiose way of talking about Tyrells lightly sea salted, but it is as true of crisps as it is, say, of a roasted lamb shoulder and minted new jerseys; more so, I'd argue, being more hands on and less nutritionally valuable. We do not need crisps, we want them. After a drink or two, they sate our desire for something salty and snackish. When we share crisps with other people we reveal not just our appetite, but our desires and susceptibility to temptation: 'Oh, go on then' we say, reaching for the remaining fragments. A few beers might make you friends with anyone for an evening – but a packet of crips seals the deal.

In part it's the complicity born of sharing something unhealthy, my friend Lauren observes over a fitting feast of almond croissant, marmite croissant and cinnamon bun, shared between two of us. Stretching and tearing the laminated luxuries into halves, we marvel at the fact we're eating pastries simply because we want to, not because we're heartbroken or having a bad day. So often in life, particularly the life of a woman, 'treat' foods need justifying to oneself and to others. Being dumped is a good one; I am even guilty of feeling secretly slightly pleased I've been dumped so I can eat an entire tub of ice cream. Yet in the hierarchy of justifications for unhealthy eating, being 'in it together' is king.

Which is why crisps are such a compelling example, being universally enjoyable and devoid of nutrients. To this day, Lauren has a long-standing conflict with her schoolfriends about what counts as a crisp, born of the days when they would try and give them up in the name of dieting or Lent. When one of their number was mid-diet, the game was to sabotage them: to casually offer a Mini Cheddar, and – if they succumbed – argue it was a crisp and they'd failed. 'We still argue about that now,' she laughs. 'Do we define crisps by the narrow parameters of being potato based, or is maize included? Don't tortilla chips count?' Yet on the rare occasions they all decided to fuck it and feast on Doritos, there was 'that really gleeful sense of all falling off the bandwagon together,' she says.

The complicity is gleeful – but there is a darker flipside, which is that that complicity is necessarily born of the guilt we feel around some foods. For Lauren and her friends to bond over binging on crisps, they had to avoid it first. 'My friend Alice was my partner in crime for some ridiculous fad diets at school, including one where for two days we ate nothing but baby food. It was a strong foundation for our friendship,' she recalls. I am reminded of my longstanding, food-centric friendship with Emma, born in year four out of our pretending to be ants in the playground, but cemented in senior school by our alternately spending five hours in the gym and eating an entire cheesecake.

Because my eating disorders continued well beyond school, several of my subsequent friendships were also forged in the fight to eat less and weigh less. My friend Stevie and I look back in amazed horror at the bizarre contortions we'd go through at university to avoid meals. After lectures on Thursdays, we'd get lunch – 'lunch' being a papaya and pineapple smoothie. Options low-calorie hot chocolate was our 'treat' in the evening. When food writers like me write breathlessly of food's potential to connect people, we forget that dieting connects us too: even Diana Henry recalls counting calories with her friend Jenny, and celebrating when they learnt the tuna niçoise salad at Pizza Express had fewer than the roast chicken one. Misery loves company, after all, and there's no misery quite like denying yourself food.

Today, though we loathe the term, Emma and I are 'foodies': in the professional sense, in that we work in it, and in the social sense in that we regularly eat and drink together. Over margaritas and long dinners in restaurants we choose meticulously months in advance, we laugh at our teenage neuroses. Now, we swap restaurant recommendations and favourite dishes. When we caught up during lockdown, we cooked 'together', laptops perched on the sideboard, and spoke longingly of where we'd go when the world reopened. We're not unusual: most people I know commune over drinks, dinner and lunches, and felt their absence keenly during the pandemic. Yet in Britain at least, this social centring on food is relatively new.

As a young person and even for most of her adult life, my grandma would never have gone for coffee with friends, still less brunch or dinner. If someone popped round, she would have offered them tea and something sweet if she had it – but she'd wouldn't have regarded it as 'entertaining', just being polite. In part this is class-based: women in the upper echelons would undoubtedly have thrown dinner and tea parties for friends moving in similar circles. But eating and drinking as a social activity for the masses didn't take off in a big way until the 1980s, explains food historian Polly Russell.

'With the setting up of Italian restaurants and cafés and then, slightly later, of Chinese and Indian restaurants, there was a democratisation of eating out,' she says. 'It wasn't just fancy hotels with French menus. By the 1980s or 90s, eating out as a leisure activity was almost ubiquitous amongst anyone with a disposable income.' Just prior to that development was the countercultural movement during the 1960s and 70s, in which young people sought to relax the social hierarchies that had existed previously. One obvious and enjoyable way of doing that was through cooking and eating together. 'People would cook big veggie chillies or soups and invite people round or go round to each other's flats and bring dishes for potluck dinners,' she continues. 'It was informal and causal; the food was the facilitator – the catalyst, even, for social encounters, far more so than eating out because it was cheap.'

Polly observes that this rarely happens now, at least amongst people of a certain demographic. Dinner parties are painstakingly plotted. The food is as much about showing off as it is bringing people together, and the big veggie chilli has largely been usurped by something complicated and ingredient heavy from Ottolenghi. There is love there, but there is also pressure to cook something interesting and in-keeping with your guest's dislikes and dietary requirements. It is easy to forget the whole point of a dinner party when one is elbow deep in potato and egg yolk hellbent on handmaking croquettes, to realise you have been so preoccupied with dinner you have hardly engaged with your friends, just as your last guest is taking their leave.

Personally, I love throwing a dinner party. But I have learnt over time that there is a balance to be struck between focusing on the food and focusing on the friendship. The relationship between the dish you cook, and the love you convey through that dish is less of a straight line and more of a bell curve. Beyond a certain point – such as making fresh ravioli for 10, a mistake that resulted in my crying and our not eating until midnight – the amount of love you feel as a result of your efforts enters a point of diminishing returns. I have had fun making elaborate meals, but that fun has been rooted in the food, not the friends I am cooking for. By way of contrast the meals in which food and friendship have felt most in sync have been those which take love and some time to make, but deliver far more time with loved ones: the pasta bakes, cassoulets, pies, one pot roasts and lasagnes with cheap garlic baguette on the side.

These are the meals we invariably grow up on, and they are the recipes many of us are sent to university with. There, in overheated halls and chilly student houses, cooking continues to be as cheap and socially constructive as it was for the counter-culturalists of yore. In this regard my university was far from typical. In the first year at Durham, we lived in college, so our meals were all catered for. That was its own leveller: you could be eating with landed gentry (indeed you probably were, in Durham) but you'd never guess from their dinner, which would be exactly the same as yours, unless you were vegetarian. Being catered for had its charms, in that the long communal tables were quickly colonised so each burgeoning group of friends had their own table, where you knew you'd find one of your number come mealtimes. Yet it was only in second year, when we moved out and started cooking together that our collective and individual identities in food revealed themselves.

Again, were you my grandma, you'd find the idea of food 'identity' bizarre, having grown up in an era where most people you knew ate the same way you did. The proliferation of cheap, mass-produced food, of different cuisines and exotic produce meant that by the millennium food, like fashion, could convey personality; that 'young people could socialise and create a group identity around the experience of eating,' as Polly observes. My housemate Pippa loved Marmite, ate with unerring regularity on account of being at boarding school, and cooked a roast dinner most Sundays along with Harry, our other ex-boarding school housemate. She drank coffee, not tea, and baked a whole Camembert whenever we had friends round – enhancing the sophistication conveyed by her crisp Ralph Lauren shirts. Ana-Rose grew up in Wales, had a slightly bohemian style, drank herbal tea and erred toward stir fries. Her contribution to the roast dinner was cheesy leeks, whilst Pippa's was bread sauce. Before going to university, I'd had neither dish, but the resulting meal – complete with my cauliflower cheese – was an encapsulation of our household. Like our now longstanding friendship, it evolved.

Of course, being four white, middle-class Brits from conventional families, there was a limit to just how much our meals could evolve through our cooking together. The same could not be said of Gurdeep, who is British Indian and shared his university house with Frank, of Turkish descent, Chloe, of Israeli parentage, and Kate, a British woman he lovingly describes as 'very well to do'. Over the ensuing two years, their eclectic way of eating merged into one, he says. 'We bought for ourselves – there was no group shop, like some houses had – but inevitably it became a joint pantry. Chloe always bought tahini, so I incorporated it into my cooking. She would make an Israeli fish stew and add amchur or tamarind from my cupboard. I hate the word "multicultural", but our palates and our pantry did become intercultural – and that shaped my cooking, because it wasn't like anything we had at home.'

That intercultural kitchen would prove formative in Gurdeep's career in food – most notably in his blog-turned-book *Mother Tongue* which explores second generation identity and migration through food stories and recipes. 'It made me excited and inquisitive about how the flavours I love can be expressed,' he enthuses. 'For example, I love things that are very savoury or sour, and I love finding that in different cuisines. I love discovering that there are people around the world who like the same flavour profiles I do, but are fulfilling them in a different way.' Where some see differences, Gurdeep sees similarities: how the use of fennel seed in Indian cooking is analogical to aniseed in Swedish cuisine, or how the

Indian dhokla, a savoury lentil sponge cake, can stand in for breadcrumbs in a sausage meat stuffing.

My own friendship with Gurdeep was forged over a discussion about Christmas dinner and the culinary idiosyncrasies of our respective families. We bonded over a carafe of wine, Italian olives, our mothers' shared mix-and-make-do approach, and the fact neither of us found our own identity in food until after university. Today, Gurdeep's 'multicultural' recipes – carrot halwa millionaire bars, mango shrikhand pavlova – are testimony to the fact that these days food doesn't just make friendships; it reflects them, too.

This isn't always as spellbinding as an extraordinary fusion dish, or even a roast dinner compiled of your respective family dishes. Sometimes it is as simple as a food or drink you always have together, like the cheesecake Emma and I shared as teenagers, or the noodles which are so central to mine and Lauren's relationship we even ate them in lockdown, broth dripping onto our laptop/computer keys. Their taste is talismanic, signifying not just a shared love for noodles, but for the comforting quality of a friendship in which we are as vulnerable about our body hang ups and career anxieties as we are about soy sauce staining our mouths and dresses. 'Nothing says friendship like watching each other eat noodle soup on screen,' Lauren remarked on our Zoom call, carefully wiping a splash from her camera lens.

Inevitably, Lauren and I being linguistically irreverent millennials, this culinary ritual now comes complete with its own set of slang words and abbreviations. Noodles are 'noods', and 'to noodle' is now a fully conjugated verb. A WhatsApp conversation might run as follows: 'We've not noodled in ages! Where shall we nood?' and the exchange serves as a sort of catechism which reinforces our relationship. The same is true of Emma and I – not with cheap cheesecake anymore, thank God, but with margaritas, which we refer to as 'margs' or 'Margaret', if we're feeling particularly spirited.

I'm sure anyone overhearing Emma and I say 'Where shall we marg?' feels it encapsulates everything that's wrong with our avo-eating, snowflaking, woke generation. Yet much like the food they reference, these linguistic in-jokes generate a strong sense of belonging. As the title of Gurdeep's book, *Mother Tongue*, encapsulates, food and language share many traits – one of which is their potential to create a clear sense of collective identity. That feeling you get when you use a word or acronym only your friends understand is analogous to you always going to the same local pub or eating bufalina pizza every time you get together. Over time certain places, dishes or foods become, like the name of your WhatsApp chat, part of the vernacular of the group.

For my 'Durham girls' group this is rosé – *blush* rosé, please; for the 'Moonwalkers', it is Pringles; for 'Fat Buddha' it is particularly thick chocolate cookies and the eponymous Fat Buddha, a Thai restaurant in Durham. So engrained do these places or foods become in one's various friendship groups, they can almost seem like a member in their own right: no gathering of the Moonwalkers is complete without Pringles and even in winter our Durham girls' group will have rosé. Some meals serve as cues for the friendship to enter a different mode. My boyfriend has a group in which, if they drink a particular Sicilian wine, they have to be entirely open with each other, whatever the question. My old housemate Katie and I had a similar ritual – its origin now lost in the mists of time – whereby we'd sit on the bathroom floor, have gin and halloumi, and talk through the fears and hopes we didn't necessarily share day to day.

On the flipside, however, food and language can also serve as tools of exclusion – often at the same time, as I have found as a food writer struggling to remember the difference between casarecce and strozzapreti. The drive to fit in is extraordinarily powerful and applies as much to food as it does music or clothes. Indeed, sometimes it feels like food has usurped the latter. Where once we flaunted our cool with CDs and gig tickets, now we signal our foodie-ness with our cookbook collections, natural wines and reservations at the latest Mexican-Japanese small plates concept. Explaining the merits of these foods or menus to friends or family who aren't foodie, who'd like their mozzarella without furikake and salmon roe, and with some bread, please, can leave both parties feeling silly – like a joke that loses all its humour for being explained.

'Well, it's this condiment of dried fish and seaweed from Japan, and it complements the creaminess of the cheese' we'll ramble to the nonplussed non-foodie, who will invariably respond by exclaiming at the price of the dish. The result is often a sense of failed connection, of the meal excluding rather than including; in short, of food doing the opposite of what food should ideally do. I love having friends in food. I love the industry gossip, the freedom to wax lyrical about a new discovery, and the mutual understanding when dinner is served that 'the camera eats first', as my restaurant PR friend Hugh perfectly puts it.

Yet of all the friends I have made through food, it is the ones I see outside of the 'in' circles I cherish most: in pubs we've picked out of love not press releases, hanging out in our respective flats and cooking crisp burnt lasagnes that will never see the light of Instagram. Food can and does make friends of complete strangers; it can fuel, sustain and signify friendship. Yet as love is what is left over when being in love has burnt away, so friendship is what remains amongst the empty plates and sputtering candles, as you chat long into the night over the dregs of the wine.

Recipe: A 90s school packed lunch

It was a rare and lucky person whose parents could both afford and allowed the full gamut of these ghastly packed lunch items. At best, Jenny, Amy and I might have three to four between us, to hog greedily or – on generous days – to divvy out. Looking back now, it seems unbelievable that these products even passed as food; yet they did, and we were delighted by them and the brightly playful and environmentally ruinous packaging in which they came.

Ingredients
Peperami
Cheestrings
Dairylea Dunkers
Müller Corners
KP Choc Dips
Babybel
Dairylea Lunchables
Chipsticks/Monster Munch/Space Raiders
Mini Cheddars
Mint Viscount/CLUB/Penguin/Wagon Wheels/Jaffa Cakes/
   Rocky biscuits
Capri-Sun/Um Bongo/Ribena
Frubes
Sun-maid raisins
White bread sandwiches with ham and/or cheese and tomato

Method

Assemble any of the above into a lunch box, preferably one with the latest cult cartoon or boyband on the front. Don't, for an all-girls school, put it in a lunch box featuring Star Wars; I learnt that s the hard way o your child doesn't have to. If you feel like nodding to health, add a satsuma or banana – but be prepared to find them squished and splayed across the bottom of your child's rucksack when they get home.

7

Melanie's Lovely Lentils

Dining across dietary divides

A year after entering secondary school, I announced I was becoming 'vegetarian', to the bemusement of my friends and the dismay of my family. I say 'vegetarian' in quotes because if I could secretly sneak a sausage or a steaming spoonful of spag bol from the pan, I would do; my eschewing meat was not the ethical choice I insisted it was, but a ploy to minimise the calories I consumed.

My decision was 'frustrating', Melanie remembers diplomatically. Though both parents and step-parents saw this for what it was, it was Melanie who did the shopping and cooking for me and the boys when we were at Dad's, Melanie who was – albeit unofficially – tasked with ensuring we all ate healthily whilst I surreptitiously traded potatoes and bread for my brother's veg. 'I think if it had been now, with so much more information and these exciting vegetarian recipes around, we'd have had more vegetarian meals as a family. I wouldn't have cooked two different meals. But back then it was just jolly inconvenient having you and then three young boys to feed,' she continues. Melanie's lovely lentils – as they became known by her friends – served us both by being cheap, quick and one of the few meals I'd eat in any meaningful quantity.

My being 'vegetarian' wasn't just practically disruptive, however; it undermined the whole dynamic of the dinner table. It upset my brothers, maddened Melanie and – if he was home – stressed my dad, who didn't know whether to pressurize or plead with me into eating something else – something more. As eating together had once connected us, so my not eating drove us apart; my demands for different dishes and smaller portions creating a distance I couldn't help doubling down on. For all our apparent fluidity and flexibility around meals these days, there remains something innately disconcerting about eating with someone and them picking about, choosing something 'off menu' or – worse – eating nothing at all.

Which is why restrictive diets prove so divisive; why, according to a recent report from *The Guardian*, vegans experience discrimination and bias on a par with other minorities. 'For millennia, eating together has been the hallmark of a refined civilisation – the thing that marks us out from the animals', says Kaori O'Connor the anthropologist, reminding me of the oft-quoted line of Epicurious, the ancient Greek philosopher: 'To eat and drink without a friend is to devour like the lion and the wolf'. Indeed, our instinctive aversion to someone not eating is arguably even more primal than that: 'Without food we would die, so there's an intimacy in giving food to another person or eating with them, much more so than with anything else we can do,' explains Kaori. To not eat is to implicitly call into question not just our intimacy with that person, but our health and mind – even our appetite for life.

These days being a vegetarian – even a difficult, disordered 'vegetarian', such as I was – hardly seems restrictive; yet it was in north-west London in the early 2000s. I had friends who avoided beef or pork for religious reasons, but veganism and gluten-intolerance were nowhere to be seen. My experiences with family and friends afforded me an early initiation into how profoundly isolating it is to eat differently to other people, whether through necessity, design or disease, which is what my 'vegetarianism' turned into. The less I ate, the lonelier I felt: at home, but particularly at school, where my studious avoidance of birthday cake, snacks and lunch left me increasingly alienated. There's no fun in asking someone on a cheeky dash to Waitrose, if the most 'cheeky' thing they choose is an Innocent smoothie of kiwis, apples and limes.

Nowhere was this more evident than at the McDonald's in St George's shopping centre, a bleak but necessary place for a teenager growing up in north-west London suburbia. Our Saturday trips to St George's were our first solo forays along the Metropolitan line, taking us three tantalising stops closer to London and all it entailed. Those who have never visited Harrow might know it for its public school, which you can just see perched loftily atop the hill of Harrow on the Hill as your train pulls into the station. Yet it is the low-slung, red-brick shopping centres St Anns and St George's that most people frequent Harrow for; and where each weekend we flexed our newfound freedom by choosing what clothes we bought, which films we watched, and what we had (or in my case didn't have) for dinner.

To miss it was to miss everything and nothing. It was to miss imperceptible shifts in group dynamics; the cumulative connections forged by sharing fries and ketchup, or choosing between a Big Mac or a milkshake. This was food that mattered not so much for what it was as for what it *wasn't*: healthy and cooked by or chosen by parents. One ate it in order to feel independent from them, and in with the group – which made *not* eating it particularly problematic. My teenage anxieties seemed almost to manifest themselves in those sweet, synthetic buns, the fiddly ketchup pots, the red sleeves of regimented chips and the Fillet O'Fish which I fiddled with under the harsh white lights of the food court. Like the shopping centre itself, caught between country and city, dependence and independence, I was neither out nor in.

It's a feeling my mum's friend Louisa can relate all too well, having been on the Cambridge diet for the best part of a decade. For those who aren't familiar, the Cambridge diet involves replacing all meals with a drink laced with nutrients and a synthetic flavour – meaning her husband Ian can quite seriously claim he's shared more meals with Freddie than with her, and Freddie is their six-year-old Yorkie-poo. They don't eat out, and they rarely have people round because the only food in the house is the food Ian buys and cooks for himself, and dog meat. She meets my mum for walks, a cup of black coffee or in the pub for a glass of tonic water – slimline, obviously.

Considering this in the context of all that I've written so far about food and love, you might wonder that Louisa has friends at all, let alone a husband. That she does is testimony not just to her excellent character, but to the way she speaks and feels about food. Louisa is half Italian. She understands what meals mean beyond the table and can talk about that at length. She reads articles about food, chats to my mum about recipes, and always asks what I am writing about. It is a telling and unsurprising irony just how enthusiastically people on restrictive diets talk, read and write about food – as if, unable to commune with their fellow diners through eating, they must compensate by incorporating it into other mediums. Melanie hit the nail uncannily on the head once when she remarked, 'Where did all that not eating get you – apart from being a good food writer?'

Creativity thrives in constraint, and I'm sure my ability and appetite for writing about food and drink stems in part from my having avoided them for so long. The human need to connect cannot be underestimated and, like water, it will eventually find a way regardless of obstacles in its path. What strikes me most when speaking to friends and family on restrictive diets (whether necessary or self-imposed) is just how determined they are to forge some sort of culinary connection with their loved ones, and vice versa: be it through articles and conversation, a slimline tonic water or finding a dish which, like Melanie's lovely lentils, can build a bridge.

When Angela's son James told her he was becoming vegan, her heart sank. Chicken soup, fried fish, schnitzel – suddenly her whole roster of family dishes was off limits. 'I knew I should applaud and commend him, but it shook me,' she confides. 'It felt like I no longer had a role.' Being a sensitive soul, James anticipated this, and was as anxious as Angela to ensure their mother-and-son bond – a bond which had been firmly rooted in food – held fast despite his decision. 'He wasn't moralistic, and he wanted to make it right.

He said to me, there are lovely things you can do, and you will do them with the same love.'

Needless to say, Angela rose to the challenge: leafing through new recipes and tweaking old ones. Though you cannot make chicken soup without chicken – she laughs at the absurdity of my question – you can make many other soups, and they are almost as good for the soul. Her willingness to flex for even the food she loved most reminds me of Grandma who, when my cousin became vegan, channelled her early disapproval into vegan cakes, looking up the unfamiliar recipes on her iPad. She drew the line at whipped oat cream (she tried it and concluded it was utterly inedible) but has otherwise continued to blend vegan block, vegan eggs and sugar together each time Joseph visits, determined not to let his dietary preferences prevent her baking for him – and by baking, being his grandma.

'Food is a way of showing love, especially for women – so when we reject food, it feels like a greater rejection,' says psychologist Amanda Hills. Like Sandra Wheatley, Amanda is a psychologist specialising in familial, child and business relationships, and someone I have known and worked with for years. When James told Angela he could no longer have chicken soup, it was rejection she felt – 'Like a knot in my stomach,' she says astutely. Yet their meals together since have gone on to prove that this dynamic between cook and eater can be a two-way street if both show willing; if both are able to, as Amanda puts it, flex to each other's tune.

Flexing is a way of showing you are someone who can be mindful of the other person – 'of demonstrating empathy through food,' Amanda continues. As opting out of a shared meal threatens to undermine a relationship, so it is bolstered by compromise; by finding a way in which both parties can opt in. This can be as simple as my grandma Googling 'vegan millionaire's shortbread' on her iPad, or as tenacious as Melanie cooking and freezing batch after batch of lentils to sustain me when my wish to be thin outweighed my ability to be reasonable. At the same time, my cousin conceding dairy cream and even the odd slice of buttered ground rice cake shows that care and consideration cuts both ways.

The most extreme and touching example of flexing for love that I have heard of comes from another of my mum's friends, Lisa, who in 2001 was given a terminal cancer diagnosis. For the ensuing 15 months Lisa followed the Plaskett diet: an extreme, vegan-based eating regime excluding salt, vinegar, anything fermented or inorganic, processed foods, sugars and all fat, which seemed pioneering and innovative at the time. Needless to say, there were scant opportunities for family and friends to socialise with her over food and drink, for long as the only coffee she could consume was via an enema. Yet her husband Simon followed the diet with her to the letter, even taking the same lunch – plain brown rice with plain steamed vegetables – to work.

That Simon decided to stand with her in this as with everything else was not surprising, says Lisa; he is a steadfast person. But even she was struck by the extent to which he stuck at it, such that the diet rendered them their own community. Cancer kept them together, Lisa tells me – but the Plaskett diet cemented them, and though after 15 months she herself concluded it was cultish, she never once heard it from him. Whether or not the diet had anything to do with Lisa getting a surprise all-clear a few months later is disputable – but having

Simon's unwavering support, manifested in his brown rice and green juices, must have helped.

In retrospect I wish I'd flexed more for my family; conceded some chicken, or at the very least not excluded bread, rice and potatoes as well as meat. Then again, my 'vegetarianism' wasn't vegetarianism so much as an incipient eating disorder, and I'm wary of conflating disease with dietary choice. Not that there isn't crossover: a diagnosis of coeliac disease doubles one's risk of developing anorexia, for example, whilst recent research has also suggested the prevalence of disordered eating behaviours is significantly higher in individuals who avoid animal products, and that veganism and vegetarianism can often mask more pathological feelings around food. In short, the difference between diets and disorders is not absolute, and that may explain why we react so strongly to our loved ones cutting a food group out of their life.

Needless to say, the reaction of Melanie and my parents to my eschewing meat had more to do with anxiety over my health than it did the logistics of grocery shopping. 'Watching your body wizen away, not getting periods or doing any of the other things your body should be doing – it was hard,' Melanie says. Harder still was her having to bear witness to my dad and brothers' suffering and feeling that, as my stepmum, she could not really lay down the law. It's a mark of just how much Melanie and I have always valued each other that the 'You're not my real . . .' bomb has never been detonated, but it doesn't need to be said for it to exert an influence. 'Of course I knew you were lying when you told us you would be eating at Sarah's house party,' she recalls, 'but can you imagine my telling you, you can't leave unless you have dinner?' Likewise at Mum's house, keeping the peace invariably trumped making a stand.

Only once do I remember Melanie losing it completely: when I refused to eat a bowl of muesli she'd soaked overnight and she threw it on the floor in an explosion of oats, milk and bone china. I was shaken, but undeterred – even glad to be shot of the muesli, the mess of which I stepped over to collect my coat before walking out. The cruel perversity of an eating disorder is that the more someone tries to feed you, the more you resist the food and sabotage your relationships, compounding the physical and psychological gulf between you.

My cousin's veganism was not a screen for anorexia. Yet observing the attitudes of others toward my eating habits has forced me to consider my own behaviour; the way in which someone's decision to exclude something from their diet can often leave me feeling affronted, as if it's a personal slight. This is particularly true if the food they've excluded has been something we've previously bonded over, like the chocolate Minstrels which were something of a leitmotif throughout mine and my cousin's relationship. As kids sharing a room at Grandma's we'd balance them on the bulb of our bedside lamp until the insides melted into chocolate pools which burst onto your tongue when you crunched them. The challenge was to remove the Minstrels before the outside candy shell softened and smeared the bulb with a tell-tale mark.

Later on, when we were starting out on our respective paths of journalist and photographer, we would join forces on poorly paid field trips for magazines like *Geographical*. Stashed in the dashboard of my cousin's fiesta was a petrol-station packet of Minstrels which would substitute breakfast, washed down with a Starbucks cappuccino. When my cousin announced his veganism, I was upset that he could no longer enjoy my grandma's sausage rolls, Christmas dinner and mandarin orange pudding. But my breaking point – the point at which I took his veganism personally – was on a research trip in Portugal, when he rejected the Minstrels I ran excitedly back to the rental car with, having found them in a corner shop.

I felt at once betrayed and depraved for having tried to tempt him away from veganism with some cheap chocolate nostalgia. My reaction was specific to our relationship – yet it was also symptomatic of the reaction vegans inspire at large. No matter the validity of the arguments for veganism, the ability of its proponents to resist the finer things in life for the greater good inevitably leaves many of us feeling inadequate – shabby, even. A SlimFast diet might inspire pity, a paleo diet a roll of the eyes, a gluten-free diet frustration unless medically necessary. But veganism introduces a moral dimension which can be hard to stomach when you want meat or dairy. If eating separate food can be potentially divisive, how much more divisive is it knowing your dining companion regards your dinner a crime.

I am reminded of Lauren's 'gleeful sense of all falling off the bandwagon together' which points toward a far less palatable alternative: falling off the wagon solo. Where the former foretells a communally hedonistic glory, the latter bodes resentment and distaste. There are certain things which feel pointless when consumed alone: alcohol, dessert and cake are obvious – but even a good steak is less enjoyable without the participation of your fellow diners. Compound that with their condemnation and that grass-fed, 35-day dry-aged sirloin might as well be a shoe in your mouth.

I got over the Minstrels. I didn't eat them but stashed them in the dashboard of the rental car for a future driver.

And whilst away from my cousin I continue to think (and eat) sceptically with regards to veganism; when we're together I try to lean in. We share recipes from Meera Sodha: a food writer who isn't vegan, but writes extraordinary vegan recipes for *The Guardian*, making her the perfect culinary medium. If we're going for dinner in London, I check out the vegan options, and I pack his favourite Linda McCartney sausages when visiting him at his home in Madrid. In return, he will rave about how much he misses Grandma's roasts, or join willingly in a debate about the best cheese for toasties. We find middle ground not in Minstrels, but in the memory of Minstrels, and Meera Sodha's cauliflower korma with cashew cream.

Melanie partly believes I stopped eating in protest: at the divorce, at her, at not getting enough attention from my parents. I don't feel this is true; as I have said, my parents divorced amicably, and I loved my bigger, better family. But it is true that for many of us with disordered eating or restricted diets, food can reflect our relationships, with what and how much we eat or are given to eat serving as a litmus test for how we feel and how people feel about us. Like the Vicar of Dibley rolling painfully from one Christmas dinner to the next, we have all eaten for love rather than hunger before – or conversely, refused food in spite of our hunger. I have gluten-intolerant friends who have been so determined not to cause offence, they've spent all night on the loo having forced down a bowl of pasta. And I have known people so preoccupied with their rules around food, they've refused a slice of birthday cake baked on their birthday specifically for them.

Before meeting her husband Adam, my friend Stevie found the degree to which the men she dated catered for her wheat and dairy allergies telling. 'Those ex-boyfriends who were tricky about that – well, it wasn't the only thing they've gone on to be tricky about,' she says. A man who cannot cope with her sprinkling vegan cheese onto her red lentil pasta is probably not going to be a pillar of patience in other concerns. By happy contrast, Adam will willingly suffer five batches of failed dairy- and gluten-free brownies or scones until Stevie alights upon a working recipe. 'Sometimes I think Adam must just want a firm scone,' she laughs, 'but the problem with dairy- and gluten-free home baking is that almost everything comes out as a crumble. Mince pies are a crumble. Cakes and scones are a crumble.' Only when making an actual crumble does she feel safe.

Adam's steadfast support of Stevie's dietary requirements has eased her longstanding anxiety that she and her needs are a problem. Where previous boyfriends would happily go to restaurants which had nothing Stevie-friendly beyond green salad, Adam will insist they find somewhere which has at least two options for her. 'He'll even go in and ask for me, whilst I lurk outside nervously,' she laughs, 'and him being more accepting of me has made me more accepting of myself.'

Though they occasionally eat separate dinners, they always eat at the same time and, where possible, the same style of dish. It's taken a while to perfect the art of timing a red lentil vegan sausage pasta bake and one made with regular sausages – but it is funny, Stevie says, how much that synergy has mattered; how overcoming each other's differences to make and eat a meal together has strengthened them, rooting them in each other and themselves.

Readers may recall that mine and Stevie's friendship was forged over Options hot chocolate – but we are now part of a wider group that consists of a friend with a nut allergy, a vegetarian and another friend with gluten intolerance. The combination leaves our options for eating out together few and far between. In recent years, we've alighted upon Mexican as the cuisine which, being based largely on corn, pulses and tequila, ticks all of our respective boxes. The sheer relief of relaxing around a spread into which we can all dive is palpable after years of rifling anxiously through allergen sheets.

For those who have never chosen or been forced to follow a restricted diet, who have never battled eating disorders or food phobias, this might sound like an overstatement. The pleasures of finally eating more or less the same food as your friends, family and partner assuming most have only one at a time are perhaps taken for granted by those who have never experienced anything else. Yet there is, believe me, a quiet power in dining across dietary divides; in finding and sharing food and drinks in which you can all partake with equal pleasure. You'd be surprised by how much easier it is to be on the same page as everyone else is if you are more or less on the same plate.

Recipe: Melanie's lovely lentils

In an unsophisticated book of recipes compiled from different members of our church congregation, Melanie wrote that these lentils are 'a contradiction in terms for many a child and adult', being delicious but vegetarian and beige. They are a classic harried-mum recipe, originally adapted from a recipe for moussaka because she couldn't be hassled with the faff of frying aubergines and making the topping. She wrote, 'As I am always buying lentils, and have a considerable store (6 boxes, to be precise) I was pleased to find a recipe even the children like. The mango chutney somehow sweetens them up, and they last forever in the fridge.' I can testify to that: many's the time I've been subject to lovely lentils of indeterminate vintage, but I have always survived.

Ingredients, for six
2 tbsp olive oil
2 large onions, diced
3 large garlic cloves, crushed or pressed
2 large red peppers (or orange or yellow), diced
225g/8oz dried puy lentils
3 x 400g/14oz tins chopped tomatoes
2 tbsp mango chutney
300ml/10fl oz vegetable stock
Salt and pepper

Method
In a large pan, gently heat the oil and add the onions, garlic and peppers. Cook gently for 4–5 minutes until beginning to soften.

Add the lentils, tomatoes, mango chutney and seasoning. Pour over the stock and simmer for 40–60 minutes or until the lentils are cooked. These are good with chicken, lamb and sausages.

8

Malibu and Pineapple

When peer pressure is a welcome guest

As restaurant refrains go, the line 'I will if everyone else is' must be up there with 'Just tap water' as one of the most oft-repeated. Sometimes it's said in reference to starters, often it's wine, most often of all, it is pudding, when chimes of 'Ohhh maybe?' 'No, no, I'm stuffed' and 'Can we have a look at the menu, just in case?' will invariably result in one chocolate fondant with six spoons. Sometimes a natural leader will emerge: the Yes Woman who knows she wants everything and will cajole others to follow suit in the (often correct) belief they're just seeking permission. At this point, woe betide the naysayer who refuses to come in on the large middle eastern sharing platter, who declines the chocolate fondant and the third bottle of Chardonnay.

In short, when it comes to food and drink, peer pressure has its feet under every table: subtly dictating what, how and how much we consume when with others. This is true regardless of gender. Female diners are the ones I'm most familiar with, but studies over the years show that everyone eats differently with others than they do alone, particularly when it comes to people with whom they identify and want to fit in. In 2016, the journal *Behavioural Sciences* ran a themed issue on Diet, Behaviour and Brain Function, in which they reviewed various studies of the social influences on eating. They confirmed that our dietary choices tend to converge with those of our fellow diners, even when we don't necessarily know them. 'Conforming to a group norm is a rewarding experience and eating with someone else amplifies the hedonic aspects of the experience,' they wrote. They also found that receiving 'positive social feedback from our peers increases expected liking'; in short, the better we feel about the people we are eating with, the more likely we are to enjoy the food.

As ever humans are an unpredictable bunch, and the way we eat and drink socially varies according to how we feel about ourselves and our companions. If we're creatures of habit or have a very defined sense of our identity in food, we're often more resistant to herd instinct, according to their report. Highly impulsive women seem less compelled to follow the crowd than those who aren't naturally spontaneous, who look, listen and wait before ordering or asking for seconds. In general, the more uncertain we feel about a social situation, the more we will look to other people to establish what's expected – and adapt our own eating accordingly. My friend Jacqueline is absolutely the habitual, defined creature who knows what she wants and eats it – or doesn't – regardless of external pressure. Pleas to go halves on a pastry or a pudding are lost on her. My friend Lizzie is more susceptible: more likely to be strongarmed by me into another glass of rosé, or a Thai takeaway with more prawn toast and spring rolls than we can eat or afford.

Being a people pleaser and a feeder by nature, these days I am more likely to be found exerting or relenting to peer pressure than resisting it – though God knows I've done that in my time. My dodging cake, snacks and lunch in my teens was only compounded when we hit 14, the unofficial drinking age. I didn't drink – empty calories – so I missed out on the gossip that arose from the house parties which I invariably left early, exhausted from not eating either. One painfully clear memory I have of those parties is of my friend James's mum making me a cup of tea, having noticed how cold and tired I was. Huddling next to the radiator with my pale, blue-tinged hands clasped around the mug, watching my friends swigging Smirnoff Ices, I felt silly – even James's mum had a glass of wine in hand – but I didn't want or even know how to join in.

Only once between 15 and university did I experience the heady delight of throwing calories to the wind and giving in to a beverage. On the first night of our post A-Levels girls' trip to Tenerife, I announced to my friends that I wouldn't go clubbing because I was too nervous, and couldn't dance. At this, Claudia drew the line. With a prescience that belied her years, she saw how my obsession was stunting my development not just physically, but mentally too – and she had no time for my handwringing. 'For God's sake, have a drink Clare,' she ordered, pouring me a Malibu and pineapple. 'We're all going clubbing. You'll dance better if you get this down you.' There was something about Claudia's energy and forthright confidence that made her and her proffered mixer impossible to resist.

What followed was not a seminal conversion to drink –
indeed I cried when they made me do shots later that night
– but it was a foretaste of what friendship can look like with
booze and food in the picture. My inhibitions down, I dived
into the late night snacks with almost as much relish as the
accompanying post-match analysis of who had got with whom.
For once, I was in: not fully, certainly not freely, but I knew the
goss and by the end of the week had even generated some of my
own, with a guy called Samuel. 'He's hot, Clare – well done!'
Claudia and Emma congratulated me, between forkfuls of hot
chips and mayonnaise – and for once, when they offered me
one, I accepted happily.

'You wanted to feel part of a group. Most people do, with
the exception of outsiders like Elon Musk,' observes Kaori
O'Connor the anthropologist, when I tell her this anecdote.
There is a reason, after all, that humans have historically put
exile on a par with the death penalty; throughout much of our
existence they've spelled the same fate. We lived in groups;
hunted, gathered, farmed and cooked in groups. Being in
meant being fed, being out meant going hungry. 'Food is
central to society's existence, because it is one of the ways
you show belonging and non-belonging,' Kaori continues.
'Anthropologically, eating with your group was not just pleasure
– it was necessity. On your own, you could not sustain life.'

Kaori's last sentence rings in my ears as I reflect on my
first term at university, which I spent navigating the riptides
of anorexia whilst trying to go with the flow socially. I'd
arrived determined to do things differently, thanks in part to
my Tenerife experience; yet the freedom to control my entire
diet meant it wasn't long before I'd resumed my old habit of

routinely skipping meals. By that point, however, I'd met Pippa, whose education at an all-girls boarding school meant she could easily spot the tell-tale signs of disordered eating. Within weeks, she was at my door with an ultimatum. She'd spoken to the rest of my newfound friendship group, who had agreed they would not dictate what I ate. They would not force me to eat more than I wanted. But unless I joined them in the dining room at breakfast and dinner time, they would send me to Coventry.

Written down and stripped of her warm, kind delivery, Pippa's words sound insensitive. I suspect Coventry wasn't even the term she used, just my memory's projection based on my Enid Blyton-esque view of her education. Regardless: the upshot was the same. Either I showed up at mealtimes, or my friends froze me out, in a 21st-century twist on the exile Kaori describes. Yet the proof of her punishment was in my showing up at mealtimes, and eventually eating with them: not much, not easily, but something. In short, the plan worked for me.

Though no anthropologist, Pippa was perceptive enough to bet that my drive to skip meals would wane when pitted against the possibility of losing the friends I wanted to be with. Smarter still – from an anthropological and psychological perspective – was her focusing on getting me with them around the same table, in the close, clattering warmth of our college dining room. There was no explicit pressure on me to eat, but the mechanics of peer pressure are such that not eating whilst everyone around me did would have been nigh on impossible. Even if all I had was grated orange cheese on broccoli (and I did, most evenings), just being there made me feel a subliminal pressure to have something.

'That's the incredible thing, with peer pressure,' says Bee Wilson. 'We talk about it as a negative thing, but the effect of social mirroring is profound and can – in the right contexts – be very positive.' She cites the example of Taste Ed, an approach to food education popular in schools in Europe, which she and others have been pioneering in the UK. The premise hinges on peer pressure: a teacher brings fresh vegetables or fruits into the classroom, and the children talk about what they look, smell and feel like. At first, they're reluctant to taste them – 'but it only takes one child and then suddenly all of them want to, particularly if that child is popular. Then it's a domino effect.'

The idea that a child's view of fruit and vegetables can be transformed though their relationship with their classmates seems revolutionary – yet it has a strong evolutionary basis, Bee tells me. 'As hunter gatherers, it would have made sense not to try something unfamiliar until we saw people like ourselves eat it, like it and survive. That is how children acquire new food habits.' They are also, as Bee observes at Taste Ed, keen to impress. Once a popular kid in a class has declared beetroot cool, their peers can't try it fast enough, so desperate are they to prove that they also like it; and whilst we might like to believe us grown-ups have outgrown that, there is endless evidence to suggest our food choices are just as susceptible to those of people we like, love or want to befriend.

It goes without saying that this isn't always positive – or rather, that it isn't as obviously positive as a class of children encouraging each other to like beetroot. Yes, peer pressure meant I ate a bit more at university and consolidated my friendships though the social fabric of mealtimes. But it made me and many others drink a lot more too. Gradually I graduated from my tame gateway drink of Malibu and pineapple to vodka Diet Coke or tonic, wine and even the Tripod: a university drink featuring three alcopops upturned in a pint glass, which left you as high on sugar as it did vodka and rum.

I regret the Tripods — but I don't regret the drinking, nor even count it as negative. Neither does Bex, another university friend who likewise didn't drink before Durham. Over cheese and a bottle of white, Bex and I agree that for all that a bond built on booze might seem sad and bad to today's more sober students, we feel it played a part in us finding our tribe. Bex was no stranger to drink, being the daughter of publicans. She grew up surrounded by it and had license to help herself if she wanted. It's just that prior to university, she never wanted to. 'I couldn't see the point. Drinking wasn't cool or rebellious. It was something my parents did. Then I got to Durham and thought, here's a group of people I love and feel comfortable with, and it was just – fun,' she recalls.

Again, this is no beetroot; but once Pandora's bar had been opened, Bex and I found the bonding opportunities afforded by booze went well beyond university. Delighted that I'd 'found' wine, my vinophilic parents took renewed pleasure in opening a nice bottle of an evening and explaining where it was from. My brother got me membership of The Wine Society, a society which he, my mum, dad and grandpa had long been part of – and I relished feeling part of that part of my family. Likewise Bex, who had never fully understood the role a good drink played in her parents' life and profession, found that now she could join them, and her family also started to feel more like her tribe.

A few years after we left Durham, Bex's mum passed away after a brief, brutal battle with breast cancer. A few years after that her dad developed kidney disease and started dialysis, so his proud Irish ability to hold his drink was somewhat curtailed. 'He didn't really drink much with dialysis – but I knew whisky was one thing he would really enjoy and savour,' Bex recalls. 'Mum hadn't liked it, so he hadn't drunk it much at home. It didn't make sense to open a bottle, though we had loads, which people had given him over the years. I knew his dad had loved it, and he and his sister and cousins bonded over it, so I trained myself to like it so I could appreciate it with him.'

Bex's dad died in 2022. Lockdowns aside, for the last five years of his life Bex spent as much time with him as possible: travelling to Edinburgh for the Festival (and the whisky), Ireland for the walks (and the whiskey), and come winter, opening up a nice bottle to sip whilst he shared many colourful stories of a life lived in pubs and hotels. 'So often the stories he told me then were of his days in hospitality, when he'd go out after work with colleagues and friends – and I was happy to have stories to rival them from nights out in Durham and London', she says. Wherever you stand on drink, there's a tangible, textural quality to this thread binding Bex and her dad – one that lives on in the collection of whisky and wine he left her, as well as in her rich memories.

Would Bex have been as close to her dad had she abstained on those evenings, had she not succumbed to that subtle, social pressure to drink with her friends, then with her family? Doubtless drink was just one of thousands of threads weaving father and daughter together. But as both Bee and Kaori have observed, there is something about sharing a physical sensation that is exceptionally unifying, especially when it is new. The beauty of food and drink is that they lend shape, colour and taste to the relationship we have with the other person, thereby rooting our connection with them in something real and corporeal. The beauty of aged drinks, like wine and whisky, is that they preserve and transcend time, better than any other drink, being the products of a specific harvest grown in a specific place and aged for a specific duration. Today, when Bex opens a bottle in the same style and age as one she once shared with her dad, its taste and aroma are an evocation of time spent with him.

On a more light-hearted note, Bex grins: 'It's cool to like and know whisky. It's an acquired taste, and I've acquired it.' Sure enough, there is a delicious, almost smug sense of belonging that comes with developing a taste for something that relatively few people genuinely like, whether it's shooting a quick smile at the chap at the bar who likes his martini with three olives, just like you like yours, or in Bex's case, having a couple of drams with her Irish cousins and proving she can hold her own. Even the idea of an 'acquired taste' is bound up with peer pressure; for what is an acquired taste if not a taste you don't naturally like, but strive to develop (with mixed success) because it will benefit you professionally or socially?

The most obvious acquired tastes are alcohol, coffee, and powerfully flavourful foods like anchovies and olives, foods which are synonymous with adulthood. Few people are born with a penchant for Pinot Gris or Gordal olives stuffed with a pimento pepper. These are flavours we force upon ourselves to impress and connect with people, in the hope we'll eventually like them: starting with milky, sugary coffee and lager, graduating to flat whites and white wine and then, as we get older and our work and friends change, pushing ourselves in still more directions – like adding extra weights to the bar at the gym.

Grimacing through skin contact wine because that's the thing our urbane friends are drinking, ordering a vongole instead of a bolognese to impress our boss, drinking espresso because we have moved to Rome, like my brother Nicholas; all these have echoes of kids trying beetroot because their popular classmates have tried it. Yet the interplay of social obligation, professional pressure and personal pride mean the workings of peer pressure in these scenarios are more insidious than anything you might witness in the classroom.

For one thing, there's more going on – and you're more aware, as an adult. This is not just about impressing or fitting in with your pals; it's about manners, cultural and social norms, other people's feelings, and the persona you are trying to convey. I speak to Bee in the run up to Christmas, and a dinner with other food writers and editors is fast approaching. 'We have to order in advance, and I'm already thrown. I'm thinking, turkey is the most appropriate thing to have but will it be well sourced enough? Will Anna Jones have the butternut squash and halloumi, and if so should I have that too? Is the vegan Wellington too boring to order?' she laughs at herself. 'It's very hard to choose for yourself in advance.'

Indeed, sometimes social and cultural pressure can force us so far away from ourselves we choose things we don't like, or that don't like us – choosing vongole even though we know the clams will come back to haunt us or shotting sambuca and knowing we'll pay the next morning. With no peer pressure at all, we would accept what our bodies told us, and choose accordingly. But we are social creatures, and our fear of missing out often usurps our biology – as testified by anyone who has ever crossed their legs tightly because the obligation to hear the end of their friend's anecdote trumps their need to pee.

If we need to feign an appreciation for fermented seaweed, or spend the night on the loo because we didn't dare say no to the cheeseboard, we will do. Amongst the long list of revered foods I've pretended to like more than I do are oysters, caviar, coriander, natural wines, Darjeeling tea, silken tofu, white asparagus, beef tartare, truffle oil, raw onion, umeboshi plums and very smelly cheese. I don't hate them. I don't gag (mostly). I'm just nonplussed, despite my best efforts. Nevertheless, I soldier through them to save face amongst foodie friends, and for the sake of the conviviality that comes with eating the same thing.

On the one hand this is a damning indictment of me and the Emperor's New Clothes attitude that prevails amongst some foodies. How many of us *do* like caviar and truffle oil, I wonder? On the other, it proves that the power of food extends well beyond personal enjoyment; that the sense of shared ceremony created by ordering half a dozen oysters and seeing them arrive on a glittering bed of shaved ice surrounded by lemons and Tabasco trumps my dislike of their taste. To turn them down would be to miss out on the whole experience, from choosing through to the chilled champagne – and besides, whilst every oyster so far has seemed slightly snotty, every oyster is different. In each gnarled grey shell there springs the eternal hope that *this* oyster will be the one that converts me.

This too adds to the joy of sharing a platter – because as Bex and her dad found with whisky, there is something uniquely unifying about tasting something neither of you have tasted before: about the expectation, about looking each other in the eye as you raise your glass or your oyster shell, saying cheers and jointly slipping the mollusc down or taking your first sip. Likewise a cheeseboard, though it does not come with a salutation, does come with a discussion about which cheese to start with, and which order to eat them in – a direction everyone follows, making the process of trying new tastes together almost a microcosm of travelling together and creating shared memories of exploring an unfamiliar country.

I think about all the wonderful, memorable things I have tried for the first time with the encouragement of other people: picking at hake cheeks swimming in salsa verde with my cousin, slurping cold biang biang noodles with Lauren, sucking the vivid red heads of carabineros with Emma, sipping my first salmorejo with my boyfriend Chris. By holding my hand or, alternatively, emboldening me to lead by example, they have enhanced my experience of the food, whilst the food and our shared memories of it has enhanced our relationship. I can no more envisage trying these foods without them there then I can touring a foreign land by myself – though to extend the analogy further, plenty of people do travel alone and meet others through doing so. This is perhaps why I have continued to try oysters with people I'd like to be better acquainted with.

It works, too. As I have expanded my palate, so I have broadened my social circle. The oyster bar at Bentley's intro-duced me to Jess and Jess introduced me to martinis, which I have happily assimilated. Through new flavours I have found new friends, and through new friends I have found new flavours – or at least I've tried to, which I think is the most important thing. In 2021 newspapers fawned over research suggesting that fussy eaters who avoid new foods are less likely to be thought sexually attractive. The study doesn't stand up to much scrutiny – the sample size is small, and the 'experiments' hardly worthy of the name – but it does reflect how I and many of my friends feel about food and relationships, both sexual and otherwise. 'No one wants to be that person, who looks at a menu and says, I can't have that or that, and I don't like that,' says Lauren. 'No one wants to be fussy.'

Lauren suffers with gastric-reflux, a chronic condition aggravated by coffee and fatty foods. That she is telling me this halfway through coffee and three pastries from her local baker Morley's does rather prove her point: she'd rather spend the afternoon feeling ill than miss out on our long-planned treat. She wants to be the person who takes fellow foodie friends to great places and enjoys them wholeheartedly, not the one who says, 'I'll have a fruit salad – but please, don't let me stop you!'

Though I can find no clear evidence to suggest this is the case, this dynamic feels more complicated for women. Social norms around food can seem in constant flux. 'Healthy' choices can be construed as rejection. Had Lauren – quite reasonably given her condition – gone for fruit salad and a green tea instead of a flat white and three pastries, would I have been just a little bit hurt? I like to think not, but we both agree that there's a mutual pact between women when it comes to eating: if one person decides to choose something unhealthy, the 'good' thing to do is to follow suit.

'I remember being dumped at university, buying armfuls of Cadbury's Fingers, and insisting my friends come to eat them with me because I am a woman and when we're heartbroken we eat this stuff,' she recalls. 'They comforted me, but they didn't want to eat them – and I felt so silly shovelling chocolate into my face. I felt offended and betrayed.' More recently, a friend with whom Lauren regularly goes for pizza spent five minutes asking for forgiveness because she'd had a huge lunch with loads of bread and she just wanted a salad for dinner, and was that alright because it wasn't a health thing, she just wasn't that hungry? 'It was ludicrous that she felt she had to make that speech – but we understood why she did; why she thought we might feel attacked by her having a salad,' sighs Lauren. There can be something very Three Musketeers about eating communally as women, and that can be a positive and a negative thing.

That, I suppose, is why we so often end up with one dessert and six spoons: to cover all bases. To mollify the weight conscious, expand the horizons of our more savoury minded friends and satisfy the desires of the sweet toothed. I used to feel embarrassed ordering multiple spoons for a few scoops of fondant. But now, the idea of all digging into one bowl strikes me as a rather lovely compromise: between allowing for the personal feelings and needs of the individuals whilst enjoying the sweet feeling of sharing a delicious experience as a group.

Recipe: Malibu and Pineapple

A poor woman's piña colada, Malibu and pineapple is not a drink you should be drinking over the age of 18, so Pippa told me. But should you find yourself in possession of some pineapple juice, some Malibu and absolutely nothing else in the house worth drinking, you could do a whole lot worse than this concoction, which will if nothing else give you a sugar rush to the head.

Ingredients, for one
50ml/1¾fl oz malibu
175ml/6fl oz pineapple juice
Dash of lemonade (optional)

Method
Honestly if you've got to the stage where you actually want Malibu and pineapple, I don't think the method much matters.

9

Belinda Skipper's Hummus

Why bread really is love

I am not really an epiphany person. I wish I was – it would make writing this book easier, for a start – but I can count on one hand the number of times I have experienced a defining moment in which I've felt conscious of a definitive shift. Most meaningful change in my life has occurred as a result of an eclectic accumulation of feelings and experiences which appear coherent in retrospect, but at the time provide no clear sense of 'before' and 'after'. Then, aged 29, on a sunny afternoon in Paris with Lizzie, I had a eureka moment whilst eating some bread.

We'd been walking all day: from the Eurostar to our hotel and from the hotel to the Eiffel Tower, which we'd climbed in bright, beating sunshine before wombling back along the slow, shimmering river. One thing we had not done was eat, bar a croissant on the train early that morning – so that when a basket of bread arrived alongside the rosé we'd ordered from a café-bar on a corner, we eagerly tucked in.

Or at least, Lizzie did. I was wary at first, knowing we'd dinner booked in less than two hours and I was still occasionally cautious of carbs, for all that I was much better by this point. In the end, though, the sight of roughly hewn pieces of baguette chucked inside a straw basket alongside small, gleaming President butter pats proved too much for my gnawing hunger to resist. I tore a piece in half, peeled a pat, smooshed the fridge-cold butter inexpertly across the soft white dough and took a keen mouthful. 'Oh my God Lizzie,' I exclaimed upon swallowing. 'I bloody love bread.'

I loved the texture of the chewy crust giving way to pillowy dough and cool, smooth butter. I loved the act of tearing and spreading it, and the deep comfort that comes with being simply but nourishingly fed. Most of all, though, I loved the sense of connection: to Lizzie of course, one of the few friends who could recognise the significance of my bread-loving outburst, but also beyond that to the long and continuous legacy of people all around the world breaking bread together; for there are few if any foods which are so symbolic of humanity and its interconnectedness as a loaf of bread.

This sounds like a lot to get out of a breadbasket, and you might well ask what about this bread prompted such a revelation? Of course, being ravenous helped – there's nothing like hunger to make the simplest mouthful feel epiphanic – as did our being in Paris, where every bar, café and restaurant serves bread as a matter of course. Though you'll find people communing over bread all the world over, in France the importance of bread to human relationships feels particularly explicit: even one of the words for friend, *copain*, comes from Latin *cum pane* meaning the person who you break bread with. In 2021 France submitted the baguette for UNESCO intangible cultural heritage status, so intrinsically bound is this bread to their society and culture. Though I had heard the phrase 'bread is love' endlessly repeated throughout my church-going childhood, it wasn't until that moment that I really grasped its significance.

Scraping the last of the President butter onto our final pieces of bread, I felt in practice what I realised I'd only known before in theory: that to break bread with friends doesn't just mean to eat with them. It means to socialise, share and chew over thoughts and experiences. It means to partake in a tradition that transcends countries and cultures; that represents civilisation, conviviality and hope. 'Going back to antiquity, the first human use of grain was to boil it up into basic porridge,' anthropologist Kaori O'Connor explains. 'To grind, clean and bake it into bread was a further refinement, which meant that very early on there was a subliminal idea that bread was the food of civilised people. It has always been more than just something to eat.'

Bread is universal, she says – but it is also often a means of creating and reinforcing a sense of identity with our community or culture. 'In ancient Mesopotamia, you'll find wonderful hymns along the lines of "We are great people, we eat bread, we live in cities",' she laughs. 'The point they were making was, they were better than people eating raw grain in caves.' We've come a fair way since then, and bread is no longer a byword for being better than cave dwellers – but you only need look at the clamouring for bread in the French Revolution or the Arab Spring to know bread and civilisation continue to be inextricable. The humble loaf is still a mark of identity for different communities. By extension, it is also a means of connecting with those communities that aren't our own.

Besides mine and Lizzie's own relationship, our basket of bread in Paris captured that spirit of international friendship and national character. The baguette is the quintessence of France and French hospitality: it's something the French pride themselves on, and which connects them – quite literally, in the queue for the boulangerie every morning – but it is also something they're happy to share. Throughout my career as a food writer, I have written for Borough Market's website and magazine. Beyond cheese and meat, bread and baked goods are probably what the market is best known for, and I have interviewed many bakers and pastry chefs in my time. To talk to any of these hard-working individuals, who slog for long hours at a time most of us are sleeping, is to receive a lesson not just on dough, but on life, love and philosophy – and the most philosophical of them all is, unsurprisingly, a Frenchman called Olivier Favrel.

At one point I was fortunate enough to visit Olivier at his bakery and see for myself the sacks of flour and the huge ovens where Olivier's magic happens. As I breathed in the scent of freshly baked boules, pain au levain and, of course, baguettes, Olivier told me the one style of bread he refuses to make is rolls. 'Bread is for sharing. If you pay attention at dinner or lunch, you will feel a little difference when people pass each other the bread – more than passing the salad, or the salt and pepper,' he said. 'There's a connection there: in the bread being touched, broken and shared around. There's no love in an individual roll.'

If Olivier wanted to make money he would make rolls, he confided, which he could charge a lot more for per unit – but he is content not making much money. He told me he feels rich enough in his wife, young twins, Oscar and Ophelia, and in his customers; and he is constantly struck by the power of baking to bring them all joy. Olivier recalled admiring his uncle, a pastry chef who would arrive late after dinner each Sunday and deposit a big cake from the bakery where he worked on the table for Olivier and the other kids. 'He would go straight to bed. He wouldn't really eat it with us – but the look on all our faces when he arrived...' Olivier trailed off, remembering, 'He was our king in that moment. It must have been like winning the lotto – but better, because those cakes made us happy. When you win the lotto, families fight.'

Intrigued by Olivier's observation that a loaf of bread generates more connection than a roll, I decide to speak to Stefan, one of his employees and something of a stalwart at Borough Market. For over a decade, Stefan has sold bread here: first at Bread Ahead, then at Olivier's, all the while studying psychology and undergoing training to be a therapist. He's loved seeing the theory of his course play out in his work at the market. 'I'm not analysing people,' he laughs, nodding over my head at a passing regular, 'but everyone, from all walks of life, buys bread, so I have a lot of rapid-fire interactions with people. I've become much better at reading emotions.' Yet it was actually in a group discussion on a weekend away with his fellow students that Stefan realised the connective power of a loaf of bread.

They'd been asked to bring in something meaningful. Stefan had been stumped at first – then alighted on bread as something both personally and universally significant, so took one of the huge pain au levains leftover at the end of the day from the stall. The time came for their show and tell, and Stefan realised he didn't have a bread knife – yet there was no way he could convey importance of bread without sharing it with the circle. Momentarily flummoxed, he broke the loaf in half, then tore off smaller pieces to pass around. At the end of a long day discussing the human psyche together, these hand-torn hunks felt more symbolic – more deeply unifying – than even Stefan had anticipated, and he tells me he strongly believes that would not have been the same had he been able to slice it up with a knife.

Stefan might have analysed that experience more than the average person, but you only need look to bread-based rituals around the world to know there is nothing new in his discovery. It's easy to forget in Britain, a country that leans toward sliced bread and secularism, but throughout history humans have favoured tear-and-share over a knife. Indeed, you don't even need to go as far as historical rituals: look at ready-made products like garlic bread, cheese bread and cinnamon buns, for which 'tear 'n' share' is a key selling point. Sure, the poetry of the Eucharist, or of the Jewish father breaking off pieces of matzo to hand to his family during Seder is more obvious, but the popularity of such products suggests something primal and enduring about the human need to physically handle their food and share it out.

As a teenager, the Eucharist in my church was always a piece of bread, torn by the priest from a large, slightly sweet, fresh loaf every Sunday. To partake of that small piece of bread was to partake of the larger body of Christ of course – I'd gathered that much – but it is what happened after the service that holds the most resonance for me in retrospect: the point when one of the youth group, usually Daniel, located the leftover loaf, brought it gleefully over, and like a triumphant hunter divvied it out between all of us.

I didn't quite know why at the time, but I loved that moment. The complicity of nicking the communion bread, the fact I was included despite barely eating, and the cavorting about that came with it fostered as much of a sense of togetherness as the official communion did – perhaps more. After all, it was more the search for friendship that led me to church than it was God, and once our own stolen Eucharist was over, most teenagers would go on to the local pub. I did not, being teetotal, so the crumb of bread torn from a loaf was the closest I came to feeling materially connected to those people. I'm not in touch with them anymore, but when Dad told me that, post-pandemic, the church had replaced the loaf of bread with pre-portioned, packaged wafers, I still felt disproportionately sad.

It wasn't the church that taught me that bread is love, though, for all the logical equivalence of 'God is love' and 'Jesus is the bread of life'. Once my Parisian epiphany had opened my eyes to the emotional power of bread, life offered no end of opportunities for it to be reinforced. There was the sourdough my brother (and every other man) made during lockdown, which we'd tuck into when it was still warm – as invested as he was in how it turned out each week. There was the extra bread an ex-boyfriend once brought and handed me under the table at a fancy restaurant because he was concerned there wouldn't be enough. There was the broa de Avintes, which Skipper, Sharkey and I devoured on sunny holidays in Portugal, bought from the bakery near the house we stayed in and broken into almost as soon as we pulled into the driveway. Tearing into the hot, dark crust and spreading it thickly with Skipper's homemade hummus, I relished my fresh lens on bread, which could see comfort and companionship rather than calories and carbs.

In short, I experienced something akin to a bread-based Baader-Meinhof phenomenon: once I'd clocked bread's role in relationships, I saw it everywhere and was continuously struck by it. I saw the pleasure wrought by my simply mopping up the remnants of a good meal with the last piece of floppy flatbread – better than any compliment, chefs told me. I learnt that the first meal new mothers receive in hospital after birth is tea and buttered toast. It was cheap, white sliced, and one of the best mouthfuls she has ever tasted, Jos assured me, after three days of labour and a Caesarean. I reread *Toast* by Nigel Slater and was struck anew by one of the first lines: 'It is impossible not to love someone who makes toast for you', written with reference to his beloved mother accidentally burning his toast each morning. With sadness, I saw how after my grandad died, my grandma shifted from loaves to rolls.

After my bread-based revelation, I went back to Mesi's Kitchen, a local Ethiopian restaurant I'd visited when I was still avoiding bread, and realised that by avoiding the injera – the huge fermented flat bread on which the curries are served – I'd missed so much more than carbs. Ten years on, Mesi can't believe it when I tell her how I'd picked the vegetable curry off the injera with a fork. 'But it's so important!' she exclaims, piling her signature selection of curries onto a huge injera for my friend Tom and I. For one thing, injera is a communal plate. Curries are dished up onto it, and everyone eats from the same injera: tearing, scooping and chatting until they reach the middle. When guests ask Mesi if they can have a knife and fork, she readily provides them – after all, she says matter-of-factly, she herself can't handle chopsticks – but usually by the end of the meal they're using their hands.

Nothing makes Mesi happier than seeing customers abandon their cutlery and rip into the injera. 'It's the eye contact. It is not just the food: it's the conversation, the feeling of sharing with your hands. It's different.' Injera feeds that feeling of kinship – but it also mirrors it, because injera on its own is very different to injera wrapped around berbere spiced beef or a gentle, herbaceous curry of yellow split peas. Unaccompanied, injera is an acquired taste. 'It's quite sour. Some people love it on its own, but most people prefer to eat it with the curries and meats because they complement each other. They are better *together*,' she smiles, her eyes twinkling at the analogy she has implied.

Like Olivier baking bread, Mesi makes injera for love as well as a living. 'Of course, you have to make money – but more of it is love: I cook the food I love, and I cook it with love,' she says feelingly. It takes two or three days to make each batch of injera, to a recipe Mesi learnt from her mother, who learnt from her mother before that. When Mesi first moved to London, finding injera was almost impossible; the only place where women were making it was an Ethiopian church. She tells me people would go to church simply to eat injera, to find an edible portal to home and family in its texture. Though injera is more common now than it was then, Mesi still feels that spiritual sense of connection to her dough, and through her dough to her country and customers – so that the love in her injera is at once communal, and deeply personal.

This feeling of kinship with the dough one is working with is by no means confined to Mesi. My work as a food writer has led me to speak to dozens of bakers, of all creeds and from all countries, and the importance of being in tune with their dough has been a defining thread. 'A chef can love their ingredients – their lamb, vegetables and so on – but I don't think they can have the same relationship to them as bakers do to their dough, because dough is a living thing,' says Olivier. 'You can't control it, and it can't control you. No one is in control, once you start the process. You do it together, feel it together – and you have to stay with it, because how it turns out will depend on what you give.'

A happy baker will make happy bread, he continues. An unhappy baker will struggle, which is why every handmade loaf is different. Of course, there are other variables, baking being a chemical process and a notoriously fickle one, at that – but there is no denying that love matters: for the starter, which needs feeding and tending; for the dough, which has to be worked with rather than against; and, crucially, for yourself. 'The ingredients stay the same. Only you change,' Olivier points out, and I reflect on that pandemic-fuelled trend for baking: how my brothers' loaves and the loaves every so-called 'sourdough bro' made during those long lockdowns may have served as covert litmus tests for how they felt.

I wonder if, subconsciously, that's partly the reason I steer clear of dough, pastry and baking in general. Until speaking to the likes of Olivier and Shuk Ng, all I knew was that my hands get hot, the dough gets sticky, and I hate it and the results. It exposes the very worst parts of me: both the baking process, and whatever excuse for a cake, bread or biscuit eventually emerges from the oven. I tell this to Shuk – an acclaimed pastry chef, you may recall – who laughs. 'With pastry, you have to find out who you are. You have to understand yourself and establish a relationship with what you are making.' In general, she continues, baking is something best done when you are happy, 'because it *is* happiness. It is something you do with yourself, but it is usually for someone else.'

Whether it's a cake, a pie, a loaf of bread or a tart, baking is a communal act – far more so than any other type of cooking. Even Grandma's millionaire's shortbread pieces, though individual to eat, are carefully cut from the same traybake – so it's the height of selflessness to offer someone the really thick, chocolatey piece from the corner. Cupcakes alone feel like the exception that proves this rule. Like rolls, they are designed for one, and their garish colours, the extravagantly tall, rich crowns of buttercream, the ludicrous mark-up all seem to point to a spirit of excess and individualism rather than generosity. Indeed, when I spoke to the founder of a local cake club a few years ago she told me they don't allow cupcakes in the club, because they cannot be shared.

As I say, I steer clear of baking – but I have always enjoyed decorating the big cakes my mum or Melanie have baked for my brothers' birthdays. Even before the advent of Instagram I cared about the presentation of food and, as baking is the most compelling example of the cooking for others, so the logical extreme of presenting food is icing a cake. It requires time, patience, and complete focus – even if it's just using writing icing, which is about as far as my talent stretches. It is warmly appreciated: your guests might not notice the artful presentation of some herb-strewn pasta, but when it comes to a birthday cake even the most basic efforts are bound to delight. It is unnecessary – no one needs cake – and it is fantastically ephemeral: as beloved and fleeting as the candlelight it is bathed in; for the moment the intended recipient blows the candles out and slices into your careful, loving handiwork, it is destroyed.

Perhaps this is why *The Great British Bake Off* has proved to be our most popular food programme, why we feel misty-eyed merely talking about Rahul's edible rock garden or Liam's 'nan' pie. To watch this motley group of amateur bakers invest so much emotion into their bakes, only for many of them to be literally and verbally destroyed by Prue and Paul moments later, is to be reassured of humanity's seemingly bottomless capacity for hope and love.

Week after week contestants lay themselves bare in their baked goods – not in the name of fortune or fame, but because they love baking for people. When they walk to the judging table with their wobbly meringues and sinking marmalade loaves, they are seeking the same happy smiles of grateful pleasure all of us hope for when we start mixing butter and sugar or kneading a dough. Their breads, pastries and cakes reflect the task at hand and their talent (or lack of); but they also reflect the mothers, grandparents, great aunts or neighbours who have inspired them, and the family and friends they have baked for. 'It touched a nerve, in that people could see how baking expresses things: expresses identity, stories, relationships. They even learn from each other,' observes Kaori, who has found *The Great British Bake Off* as anthropologically interesting as she has entertaining. 'It is a very lovely programme.'

Lovely is the word, says Lauren, who for the first eight years of *The Great British Bake Off* penned a write-up of each episode for *Grazia* magazine. 'It's not elitist. It's not challenging: we've all baked a cake before, even if we've not done so since childhood. Everyone is lovely to each other, and we watch it to watch everyone be lovely. It is the antithesis of most reality TV.' Lauren also believes the fact no one goes on it believing *Bake*

Off will change their life is one of the programme's key selling points. 'Whenever there's a montage of what the winners are doing now, they've mostly gone back to their ordinary lives. They might sell cakes every second Tuesday at the village hall but that's about it.' Even Nadiya, *Bake Off*'s most commercially successful contestant by far, is beloved because she is so loved: 'because she has this very supportive husband, who adores her and championed her and encouraged to go on *Bake Off*, and then made the most of everything that came from it.'

In a nation that feels more divided than it has ever felt in my lifetime, where culture wars rage, and 'isms' of all kinds rise, *Bake Off* has stood alone as a point of unity. You and I might disagree on Brexit, female loos, whether to mow your lawn in May, climate reparations and imperial measurements, but there are very few of us who haven't watched through their fingers as a contestant's tiered cake has collapsed, or cringed in recognition at a soggy-bottomed tart. Where the morality of the world outside of the *Bake Off* tent seems contentious and equivocal, within its canvas walls we find consensus. The moral code's unwritten but feels it right: we want the talent to be rewarded, we want hard work to be recognised, and we want people to be lovely because we know that that's what baking is; because whatever your creed or country, bread is love.

Recipe: Belinda Skipper's Hummus

Though I have only ever tried this hummus as made by my friend Emma Skipper, it is in fact her mum Belinda's recipe, and a staple of the Skipper household.

Ingredients
1 x 400g/14oz tin chickpeas
1 clove garlic, or more, to taste
Juice of 1 lemon
Salt
Olive oil

Method
Blend the chickpeas (and their liquid), garlic and lemon juice together. The more powerful the blender, the better. Salt, to taste, and add more garlic if desired. Serve in a bowl with a generous slug of good-quality olive oil drizzled on top. Belinda doesn't add olive oil into the blended mixture and neither does her daughter, so as to avoid it becoming claggy or drying out. Serve with fresh – ideally Portuguese – bread.

10

Jay Foreman's Challah Bacon Sandwich

Feasting and fasting for – and against – faith

My Parisian epiphany with Lizzie might be my most significant memory of bread, my memory of Daniel doling out the end of the communion loaf my most poignant. Yet the dough-based memory that delights me most is of my brother Nicholas making a gun-shaped loaf in Sunday school, during a baking session to commemorate the miracle of Jesus feeding the five thousand with two fish and five loaves of bread.

Even though as one of Sunday school's more senior pupils I'd been helping the little ones all morning, I'd barely seen Nicholas. A quick glance had been enough to assure me that the task of kneading the dough and shaping it into 'something you love' had him unusually rapt. Only when the risen breads emerged from the oven for each child to identify and take home did I realise how literally my brother had taken the instruction – to the dismay of the leaders, the amusement of my parents and the delight of his peers.

Fast forward 15 years, and that loaf proved prescient – not of his love for guns, but of his lack of love for religion. Though Nicholas, like me, joined the youth group at the church where my dad married Melanie, by the time he was 14 he was on to Darwin's *Origin of Species* and Dawkins' *God Delusion*. His bedside Bible had been usurped. He made clear in his life what he had indicated in his loaf: that he had no time for the strictures of religious conformity. He enjoyed the food, enjoyed the singing, enjoyed or at least respected the stories. But beyond basic morality (which he didn't need God to help him grasp, he reminded us) he had no interest in being told by the scriptures what was 'right' or 'wrong'.

It's tempting to see Nicholas's gun-shaped bread as an early act of individuation within a faith that sought to confine him. It wasn't; he was a small boy going through a fighting phase, and would have shaped bubble bath into a gun if he could. Nevertheless, the small, comic example feels illustrative – not of my brother, as such, but of the tension that often exists between food as a means of relating to ourselves and other people, and food as an article of faith.

On the one hand food can be deeply symbolic – in Christianity, but even more so in other faiths, in which the eating or not eating of specific foods is far more interwoven. Growing up in north-west London, I was fascinated by the culinary rituals of Judaism, Islam and Hinduism (three of the main faiths in that area), all of which were much richer than a sip of sweet wine and a wafer of bread. I loved the significance invested in the matzo at Passover, sweetmeats come Diwali and biryani come Eid, the feast at the end of Muslims' month-long Ramadan fast. As my friend's Vivek's mum Jayshree observed, when I spoke to her about cooking for Hinduism's various religious festivals, 'What's with Christianity? You guys only really have turkey and bread.'

On the other hand, food and drink are fundamentally worldly. Man might not be able to live on bread alone, but he certainly can't live without it. Eating is more of a reminder of our connection to this life and the people in it, than it is of the next. One of the reasons we eat at funerals is to remind ourselves that we're alive and they – well, it depends on your faith, but they certainly aren't there tucking into the sausage rolls. However much spiritual symbolism you surround a meal with, it is inherently human – which I think is why people attend religious feasts long after they've lost their religion. There is plenty of love to be found in your aunt's Simnel cake or in the fragrant depths of your grandma's biryani, without necessarily believing in God.

Nicholas's gun bread is no biryani; but it is a small, comic example of how the significance of religious foods can remain even if God is lost or lost in translation. Nicholas's joy in creating it and in presenting it to his family to eat with him mattered despite, or perhaps even because of, the religious context – for in creating it in the image of something he loved at the time, he was (though he cringes now) expressing himself. My friend Jay Foreman also grew up in north London, in a Jewish family that observed Friday night Shabbat and all the festivals religiously. Every Sunday morning he went to chedar, the Jewish version of Sunday school. Yet by the time I met him he was a self-described 'massive atheist', who at a party once told me about the decidedly non-kosher bacon sandwich he and his brother make using challah, the sweet Jewish bread.

'They go together so well because the bacon is crispy and the challah is soft, and it feels very, very naughty because obviously the challah was – well, the challah doesn't know it's heading toward a bacon sandwich,' he grins. Were Jay going out to buy his own challah and sandwiching it with bacon it would be one thing – but he isn't. The challah he uses is the same hallowed challah his parents buy for Shabbat on Friday night, which Jay still observes for the sake of the food and the family time. 'My parents will say, "Here you go, have a challah to take home with you." "Oh wow, thank you so much," I'll say, and I'll take it home. And the next morning when I'm back in my flat, I'll want a bacon sandwich and I've got the challah on me.'

Of course, the original context of the challah is important: the prayers, the Friday night gathering, the connection with Jewish families around the world and across the ages. Challah is inextricable with Jewish identity, to the point where to call it bread instead of challah would be inconceivable, Jay tells me. 'No family in the universe when they're having Friday night dinner calls it bread. It's challah.' It can only be bought from a proper Jewish bakery, because supermarket versions aren't as good, on a Friday morning because it doesn't last long; and it's only eaten after some blessings that take around three and a half minutes, but felt 'excruciatingly long' to him as a child, counting down the seconds until that first bite.

Yet when Jay and his brother commit the blasphemy of adding bacon the following morning, challah is transformed to reflect not just Judaism, but his relationship to Judaism; his transition from being devout, to regarding religion as synonymous with family – nothing more. 'There definitely was a time I would have been kind of embarrassed and want to blend in and be normal, not eat this mysterious Jewish food. Now, as a grown up, I'm very happy with my relationship with my religion – by which I mean all the Jewish cultural references: the challah, the smoked salmon, Woody Allen films – but not believing in God,' he says. 'For me, the Jewish food that I grew up with and loved – it's not a religious thing, it's a family thing. Those two words, religion and family, they're kind of the same for me.' With the addition of bacon, challah has gone from something abstract and religious, to something delicious and personal to Jay and his brother.

I am reminded of my friend Sophie, another non-believing Jew, whom I was with when she tried her first pork pie on holiday in Southwold. I watched as she marched down the crowded high street devouring it like an apple, and it felt like such a life-affirming act – not of renunciation, so much as an individuation of Sophie and her faith. Sophie's first prawn was prompted by her second (gentile) boyfriend and again it seemed food served to delineate her relationship with God, versus her relationship with him. Perhaps auspiciously, she did not much like the prawn. Bacon is one thing, she observed at the time, but shellfish is a particularly strange thing to get your head (and mouth) around if you barely encounter it until you're 18.

Like Jay, Sophie feels a strong familial connection to the culinary rituals Judaism entails – and with that, a poignant sense of nostalgia. Both Jay and Sophie are acutely aware that their secularism threatens the survival of these foods and traditions – to which end Sophie has been learning how to make salmon rissoles with her mum and, during lockdown, partook in Passover with her family over Zoom. More than prayers or hymns, food provides a tangible means of being connected to one's community and religious roots, even when one no longer believes in its orthodoxy. It goes without saying that this is particularly important to a religious group as persecuted and scattered as the Jews.

Of course, all food has the potential to connect across time and space – but religious food is a particular source of consistency and continuity, because the same dishes are made for the same festivals and rituals. Even if neither of us can recall the names of all the disciples, there is still something special about seeing a Simnel cake around Easter in the house of another vaguely Christian friend. The most powerful example of this earthly transcendence again comes from Jay, who recalls a family holiday to Brazil during which they met some distant relatives for the Passover meal, Seder.

'I love the traditions that have been passed down from generation to generation unchanged. Each family does it slightly differently,' Jay tells me. 'For example, in Seder, there's a ritual where you have a bowl of cold salt water with a hard-boiled egg crumbled into it. It's exactly as disgusting as it sounds, but you enjoy it at the time because it's part of the meal. In our family, the boiled egg goes in the water and it's our responsibility to chop it up with a spoon; someone else I know says their egg comes pre-crumbled. One of the weirdest and most amazing things was when we met some very distant relatives in Brazil for a Seder, because we happened to be there in April, and they were doing and saying pretty much the same thing we did. We realised that they've been taught to do this by exactly the same people that taught us,' he marvels. 'It takes a couple of generations on different continents for it to vary just a little bit. But it's ultimately come from the same place.'

For such traditions to die with their generation would be terribly sad, Jay acknowledges – so he's relieved his cousin has picked up the baton for the next generation. Unlike my friend Sophie, Jay has no intention himself of learning the recipes or rituals, so when his cousin hosted Passover recently it was 'such a good feeling – like yes, we're fine. It'll carry on,' he says. 'For the first time it had been passed down.' I am reminded of Jayshree making Indian sweets with her daughter Nish, and describing to me her relief that, even if she barely made them, Nish at least had the recipes. 'You don't want those skills to go,' she explained. 'Shop-bought is not the same.'

Again, I'm struck by how the significance of religious food lies more in its continuity and connection with others than it does a deity, even for believers. For Jayshree, one of the joys of making festival food is spending time with the other women, experiencing a sense of unity which the occasion necessitates, but very rarely eclipses. Cooking the milk, crumbling the egg, breaking through the dough-sealed lid into the biryani – these are precious moments, rich with symbolism. But even the most devout must surely delight in the communality of these rituals, and the way they regularly unite those friends and family members who come for the food more than they come for the faith.

Perhaps this is why so many faiths encourage fasting as well as feasting: because no matter the religious significance invested in food and drink, they are a distraction. They are enjoyable – so enjoyable even the non-believers get on board, whereas the complete sacrifice of food is the preserve of the devout. Jay might eat challah at home, but he isn't going to give up bread for matzo – the flat cracker Jews eat when they're abstaining from leavened bread during Passover – unless he's at his parents' for the Friday night meal. I've no statistical evidence, but I'm willing to bet that most people eating chocolate eggs at Easter have not given up anything for Lent.

Indeed, though still notionally Christian, I am one of those people. I toy with the idea of Lent each year but can never quite commit to it. Besides, my experience of doing Lent as a child and a teenager does not suggest it will bring me any closer to God – quite the reverse. When I compare notes with my friend Daisy who, like me, was raised in a Christian household, she says she wishes the experience of fasting had made her more spiritual – but in reality it did the opposite. 'My relationship with my body and with eating was the thing that took centre stage, rather than my relationship with God or the less fortunate,' she tells me when we meet for a drink in the run up to Christmas. Though eating in company brings her closer to people, far more than any of her other 'big loves' – books and music – going without didn't bring her closer to those who have no food. 'It just made me self-obsessed, which doesn't feel like good faith.'

Of course, Daisy and I are not a representative group. For one thing, both of us struggled with eating disorders – which made us really good at fasting, but for all the wrong reasons. It seems unlikely Jesus spent his 40 days and nights in the desert assessing his thigh gap, wondering how many pounds he'd shed. There is a logic that appeals to both of us about a period of famine before feasting – but it's hard to know if that is faith, or a hangover from disordered eating. As Daisy darkly puts it, 'Bulimia is basically a fucked up, traumatic horror-show version of Lent and Easter.' Today the only thing she gives up for Lent is alcohol, which doesn't bring her closer to God, but does bring her back in touch with who she is and how she feels when she doesn't have the option of losing her feelings in a large glass of red.

Some weeks after my conversations with Jay and Daisy, I speak to Lizzie's dad, Charles: a smiling, kindly vicar who has always been invitingly open-minded. Intrigued as to his take on faith, love and fasting, I relay some of what we have been discussing. He listens carefully before making the case that, so long as it's not being fuelled by disorder, denial is 'a good discipline that is as much a part of being human as it is a part of faith.' For Charles faith *is* love; not just for God but for other people, and fasting should mean finding the best way to act on that affection. The act of abstaining – from food, drink, or certain habits – ensures we aren't so in thrall to one thing that we lose sight of our power to help others as well as ourselves.

'When Jesus is in the desert for supposedly 40 days and he is hungry, he wants to turn stone into bread. This makes him think about how he can best use his power: for the good of others, or for the good of himself. I like to think our Lenten discipline should flow out of this recognition that we have the ability to behave selfishly, and the ability to help others,' Charles continues. One could turn stone into bread for their own instant consumption, or one could hold out in the hope of feeding five thousand people out of five loaves and two fish.

I love this perspective, and the way it unites the personal, social and religious potential of fasting. Seen through this lens, Daisy's reconnecting with herself by abstaining from booze for Lent is as valid an outcome as Charles's more traditional eschewing of meat and eggs. 'They are all part of the same picture. It helps us to understand that we shouldn't become slaves to anything, edible or otherwise, and doing that helps us think about our behaviour,' he continues. It's a far cry from fasting to binge on five chocolate eggs come Easter Sunday, or fasting to lose weight.

Listening to Charles, I am reminded of the time Sophie and I visited Jordan during Ramadan, the month-long Muslim fast, which forbids eating from sunrise to sunset. Outside of hotels, most restaurants wouldn't serve food until sundown and the adhan call which signalled the end of the fasting day. Tables groaned with the waiting meal – bowls of hummus glistening with olive oil, luminous pickles, ful medames, falafel and floppy flat breads – and as the sun slipped behind the buildings even the air seemed to vibrate with the collective restraint and anticipation. I marvelled at the kindness we had received throughout that trip from people who should have been 'hangry' yet were hospitable; and at the fasting which seemed to unite people as much if not more than the feast at the end of the day.

It's like TV used to be, I remarked to Sophie. Once upon a time we all waited for the next episode of our favourite show and when it finally aired, we tuned in and watched it as one. We might have led different lives in different parts of the country, but by watching *Friends* on a Thursday evening we were united in the same time, place and sense of expectation. Fasts and feasts like Ramadan and Passover provide a communality of experience that we rarely get in these days of on-demand streaming services – a communality that is all the greater for being steeped in our heritage.

Such is the universality of the feeling that surrounds the revealing of the matzo during Passover, Jay can't believe there isn't a special word for it in Yiddish. 'It's an experience that every Jewish person has in Passover, and it happens precisely once a year when you have the Friday night ceremony where you uncover the cloth, which would normally reveal a challah, but you reveal a matzo instead. You lift the cloth and it's there: flat, flavourless and horrible, and that's the moment of the year when you miss bread the most. There's nothing quite like the disappointment, and we all have it,' he laughs. 'Yet I also like it, because it reminds me of a fun time of year when the whole family gets together.'

I envy those moments of oneness, to which Christmas and Easter cannot really compare being more commercialised, often secular and generally abstracted beyond any religious or cultural value. Though both entail feasting with family and friends, there is no one precise, magical mouthful where you feel connected to people you love, or those you don't know but who share your heritage or faith. The Eucharist – when the leftover communion bread is not stolen by Daniel after the service – is more about you and God than it is you and your community. Listening to Jayshree describe the various foods that Hinduism assigns to life events and festivals, I am struck by how focused they are on family – as much if not more than on any deity, it seems to me.

There are the sweets made to welcome newborns – pedas for boys, jalebis for girls. There's the ceremony of Shradh, a part of which involves cooking the favourite dishes of ancestors who have passed away. In a similar vein, there is the extraordinary tradition on the first day of Diwali, where food is made for deceased relatives and left on a crossroads near where they lived – Edgware, in the case of Jayshree's former in-laws, for whom she was obliged to do this when she was married. 'You can't look behind you after you drop it off. If you look back, the theory goes that their ghost will follow you,' she explains – and we chuckle at the thought of her leaving a Tupperware of curry on a street corner in north London and scurrying away without a backward glimpse.

In comparison to all this, Christianity's cupboards feel rather bare. I say as much to Charles when we speak, and to my surprise, he partly agrees with me. 'Christianity's reputation is not a foodie one. The bread and wine is theologically central, but it's separated off. We share bread and wine in church, but we share it symbolically.' Beyond the Eucharist and Lent, food has no ritualised role in unifying Christians – and yet, when it comes to the gospels, food is everywhere, he observes. 'The only miracle that appears in all the gospels is the feeding of the 5,000. Jesus received criticism for dining with tax collectors and sinners. And of course, there's the Last Supper! Jesus was a man who enjoyed having food and drink in company.'

Reflecting on this and incorporating food and drink into his community beyond the church has been an ongoing project for Charles and ministers of his mindset. 'What's happened in my experience both as a church member and minister is that food has become more and more important as a means of meeting, sharing in and celebrating our community. We meet in church to pray, sing and be taught, then we meet afterward for a good chat, coffee and biscuits. It's not integral to our worship, but it has become part of what we do as a family, and I think bringing food into this frame is faithful to Jesus's teaching.'

When preaching about the feeding of the 5,000, Charles is fond of explaining how this beneficence is but a foretaste of the meals that await us in heaven. 'You might be surprised to learn that biblical references to what heaven will be like mostly reference food. There is no mention of harps or angels. Heaven's a feast, which we're invited to,' twinkles Charles – making the idea of the afterlife sound more like his vicarage in the village of Bovingdon than the exclusive club it is commonly seen to be.

There, the invitation to tea permanently stands. So long as he or his wife Philippa are at home, his parishioners are welcome. One year in my twenties I found myself unexpectedly alone in London for Good Friday, and no sooner had I mentioned this to Lizzie than I was on a train bound to Bovingdon for a feast of red wine, lasagne and garlic bread. Charles sang a quick grace, and we tucked into a dinner that seems in hindsight to have encapsulated so much of what he has told me about food and faith. Though I had met Charles and Philippa only a handful of times before that Friday, and am at best an inconstant Christian, theirs was a feast I was readily invited to; the lasagne miraculously doubled last minute in order to accommodate me. I felt food as the lingua franca between family, friendship and faith.

Recipe: Jay Foreman's Challah Bacon Sandwich

To be made and gobbled in secret – if your parents are religiously observant Jews – on a Saturday morning, with the challah from the night before. If you/your parents aren't religiously observant, you can make it whenever you want – though bear in mind that challah's hard to purchase at any time other than on a Friday.

Ingredients, for 1
Friday night's challah
Smoked bacon
Brown sauce

Method
On Saturday morning (it has to be Saturday morning, or it won't be fresh) slice a big chunk off last night's challah. To get a flat edge, you may need to discard (eat) the bobbly bit from where it was ripped by hand in the ceremony. Slice a second piece. It will be wonky and not the same size. This is fine. Fry some smoked bacon when your dad is definitely not looking, and eat the sandwich, dunking it in a blob of brown sauce and the remaining bacon fat in the pan. Take 20 minutes to clear up all the challah crumbs you made while slicing. You have 24 hours to graze on the rest of the challah before it becomes inedibly stale.

11

Grandad's 'Scallops'

Mourning meals

My grandad died on the first Friday of 2020: quietly, resolutely, holding my grandma's hand as he checked out of this life and into the next one. I wasn't there, but in the cold, sad pall that followed his passing my mum told me of the moment hunger hit for the first time in the days they'd spent at his sickbed. 'Suddenly, hunger rushed in' she said, of that ravenous feeling the living often experience upon losing a loved one; and this being Friday, at my grandparent's house by the seaside, there was no question around what my mum, David, grandma and aunt needed: it had to be fish and chips.

It has been thus every Friday: at my mum's childhood home in Cambridgeshire, at the hotel and at this house on the South Downs to which Grandma and Grandad retired in their seventies. Together they'd fetch huss, cod or haddock from the fishmonger, then Grandad would peel and chop potatoes for the fryer. Sometimes he'd make 'scallops': thin slivers of potato

– the bits leftover once the chips had been cut – battered and fried into crispy, oily discs. For most of my grandparents' lives this was what 'scallops' meant.

My family didn't make fish and chips this time. They picked some up from the seafront, drove home, and ate them straight from the paper with what Nigella described in her book *Feast* as 'the greedy appetite for life' that follows a loved ones' passing. I remember reading that chapter – on death and funeral food – with morbid interest as a teenager, but it is only since experiencing loss myself, and witnessing the grief of bereaved friends and relatives, that I've come to appreciate food and drink's role in helping us process the life-changing force of death.

My grandad's wake was a quiet one. He didn't want 'fuss', by which he meant he didn't want a service or any sort of big party. We remembered him by gathering together as a close family, playing his favourite card games and eating takeaway Thai from my grandparents' go-to place in East Dean. The following day we went to the Grand in Eastbourne, the posh hotel to which my grandparents would go for afternoon tea on special occasions, but to which Grandad would take his own teabags because he didn't like the 'fancy' tea they served. Only a few days before he died my cousin Joe had taken my grandparents there for afternoon tea as a Christmas present, and Grandad had, as usual, reached in the front pocket of his shirt for his secret teabag.

It was not the wake I wanted. I wanted a service, a celebration, a means of mourning him collectively with his friends as well as his family. Yet in its simplicity, intimacy and lack of pretention, it was the perfect reflection of my grandad: the

Sheffield-born railway man cum hotelier whose large, gentle hands had never done anything more aggressive than beat us at whist; who right up until the moment he passed was a pillar of constancy. 'The funeral meal is both a tribute and a final sharing with the person who has gone,' says Kaori O'Connor, when I ask her for the anthropological take. 'That is the same in all cultures.' What varies, she says, is what you eat and drink, and the degree to which the feast turns riotous: reflecting the cruel and emotionally inconceivable way in which death destroys our attempts to impose order on the chaotic experience of life.

'Everything is broken. Everything is reversed. The world is upside down and terrifying because death is the ultimate destroyer of order, and you confront that with your own display of disorder,' she tells me. My grandad's wake was not disordered – not by today's standards, and certainly not by the standards of ancient funeral rituals, in which people might take off all their clothes, dance and shout as well as drink excessively. Christianity and civilisation in general stamped many of the more extreme antics out, Kaori continues, so that today the only real source of anarchy at Western funerals is alcohol. Yet whilst I don't wish my grandad's funeral had been wilder – not least because my grandma is pointedly teetotal – I do see the merit in mimicking some of the madness of death at the feast.

One wants to freeze time: to stop all the clocks, as the poet Auden so memorably put it. In the right time and place, food and drink can do just that. They focus your senses, and with that your experience of the passing of time. They can, for the moment they are in your mouth, somehow both accentuate and disrupt the feeling of grief. This is particularly true if they are foods beloved of the person you are remembering. At her father

Dave's funeral, Jos served sandwiches filled with dressed crab or prawns, and baked a lobster-shaped cake in memory of his love for seafood – particularly lobster. Everyone wore something lobster related – socks, earrings, ties, even an entire lobster suit – and approached the sandwiches and the open bar with such spirit, it was as if we were trying to recreate Dave in his absence. Emotions during the service were raw; Jos's mum had passed not many years previously, and Dave had died shortly after she learnt she was pregnant with her first child. 'Then afterwards people are eating and reminiscing and looking at photos, and it's like an inversion of the amniotic fluid,' Jos told me. 'The food and drink become a continuation – an embodiment of that person's life.'

When Bex's mum Elsa passed, the wake took place in the pub her parents owned – and for as long as people were propping up the bar their glasses were filled with pink champagne, Elsa's favourite tipple. 'It was the most expensive party we'd ever thrown,' Bex remembers. 'Dad said, "We are celebrating your mum, and why would we spare any expense on that." Mum was always a very good host herself. She'd be pouring the wine whilst Dad was buying it. The party was full of love and booze and hospitality, because that was what she was full of.' The bitter-sweet irony of Elsa's or indeed anyone's funeral feast is that the person who would have loved it most is the one person who is missing. 'Everyone she had ever met was in the pub she'd spent a decade in, eating hearty food – we're northerners, after all – drinking her favourite drink and having a good time. She'd inadvertently hosted the best party of her life.'

It was a celebration – and a funeral feast should be a celebration, Kaori says. Yet in order for it to be a celebration of life, the presence of death has to be acknowledged. 'People aren't very good at thinking about death in this country. We'd rather deny it,' she continues. Yet doing that can risk turning the wake into little more than 'a decorative tea party, with an assortment of strangers wondering what they are doing by the sausage rolls.' In truth, the party after the feast has as much, if not more power than the service to reconcile our relationship with the departed and spark our appetite to go on living. This observation comes, somewhat surprisingly, from Lizzie's dad Charles, the vicar: 'When we lose someone we are grieving, and we are reminded of our own mortality. The instinct is to crawl off – but instead we get together and share food and drink.'

For Charles, the wake is often where the most useful pastoral conversation goes on. 'The talk is freer over sandwiches,' he smiles. 'Before the funeral it is all practical planning, which takes place in a strained context. After the service we've done the part the family were most dreading, and the food and drink enable a sense of palpable relief.' For Charles, the quality of the food is largely irrelevant – and in fact at many Christian funerals the food *is* fairly unimaginative, he acknowledges. Whereas at Jewish and Islamic funerals the food following the burial is prepared by friends of the bereaved family, at Christian funerals the catering falls to the family themselves, which means it's invariably (and understandably) outsourced to catering companies.

There is no particular significance to the sausage rolls, crisps, quiche and finger sandwiches that frequent a traditional Christian funeral; not like Judaism's salty herrings which represent tears shed in memory of the departed, or Islam's sweet halva, baked to salve death's bitterness. I'd love it if there was; if the fridge-cold quiche Lorraine was in fact symbolic of life's fragility, say, and the importance of binding to each other like egg to bacon. However, I think Charles is right: the quality or variety of the food doesn't undermine the significance of our having and sharing in it, and some people may even value such food more for its genericism: for being familiar, predictable and – contrary to the nature of the event – utterly unchallenging.

Besides, the potential of food and drink to sustain our relationships with those we've lost extends well beyond the meal after the funeral. I wasn't at the fish and chip supper my family had immediately after Grandad died. I rarely went to the Grand Hotel with my grandparents. But I was – I still am – the only person in our family who takes their tea the same way my grandad did: strong and milky. It became our catechism: every time we made each other tea, we'd present it proudly, saying 'This is the strong and milky one'. I even bought him a teaspoon engraved with the words, which he kept by the Teasmade in their bedroom. Only we understood that 'strong and milky' isn't a paradox: the bag is brewed, then plenty of milk is added, and the combination makes for our perfect cuppa. I am connected to him via this ritual just as my brother is via the ginger snaps, which he buys here, takes back to his home in Rome, and dunks just like Grandad used to do.

These are living memories. Some memories fade with distance from the day our loved one died, but food memories endure – are indeed renewed each time a certain meal is cooked or mouthful taken. This is in part why, for all its seeming simplicity, inherited kitchen equipment can carry so much emotional weight. The cocktail shaker I inherited from

Grandad is one of my most prized possessions: I know it is something he held and used, and shaking it feels like a direct connection, though he only made a handful of cocktails during my lifetime. More poignantly still, when Jos cooks with her children, she cooks with the same wooden spoon she used when she was small and cooking or baking with her parents.

Understandably, Jos sometimes struggles to access memories of her mum and dad, and relay those to her children without getting upset herself. However, she tells me she can 'touch them both through cooking because I am following the same recipes, following my senses, doing the same thing I did with my parents, and which I have always done since.' The repetitive motion prompts memories, which gather form and substance like a roux emerging slowly from the mix of flour, milk and butter. Indeed, Jos's go-to means of cooking out her sadness is to make a roux, which she describes as analogous to making sense of grief.

'I cook to think. I cook to soothe. I cook the flour out, and I'm in the moment.' It's a productive sadness, she continues, because it calms her, connects her with her parents, and ultimately provides something to eat. It transforms the kitchen into a safe space: for her to talk, and for her children, Jack and Eva, to ask about two people they have never met, yet who were formative in their mum's life. She's engaged, but not distracted; there is limited eye contact, which makes hard conversations easier, and Jack knows he can connect to his grandparents through whatever they are doing in the kitchen. At present, Eva is too young to help cook, so Jos sits her up on the work surfaces to watch them stir, chop and knead – just as her parents used to do with her as a baby.

'Jack will say, "Did Grandpa do it like that? Did you make this together?" It's a setting in which he can ask me about them, and I feel comfortable talking. I can't always open a photo album and go through it without getting upset, but I can make fish fingers', says Jos, showing me photos of Jack holding up his breadcrumb-covered fingers and grinning. For some people, it's books; for others it's paintings, clothes or furniture. My brother was delighted to inherit Grandad's fishing rod. Yet for a great many families, it is the recipes that connect them to the relatives they've lost, and through which they can feel a sense of continuity.

These recipes might be written down, memorised or penned into the margins of cookbooks covered in scribbles and stains. Jos's mum's recipes are stuffed into the plastic wallets of a lever arch file which, if she lost, would be 'so much worse than any photo album,' she says. My late step-grandmother stuck the recipe for her granola onto the top of the ice cream tub in which she used to deliver it to my brother Alexander, and where it remains for him to follow and fill. These recipes serve as a sensory route map, unlocking the touch, scent, sight and taste not of the person who has gone, alas, but of memories associated with that person. 'When I'm teaching the children to make fish fingers, I know all their senses are awakened and engaged,' says Jos. 'I know they're going to remember it.'

My grandad did not leave a recipe. He did not cook, really, beyond potato scallops. He peeled, washed up and microwaved the condensed milk for Grandma's millionaire's shortbread, but like many men of his generation his talents were better suited to the garden. There he had beetroot, potatoes, trailing rows of fruit bushes and a rain-streaked greenhouse in which, come spring, he could spend hours at a stretch. Though Grandma herself is a keen gardener, the greenhouse was Grandad's domain: warm, quiet and filled with the tendrilled tomato plants he lovingly tended. Grandma could never understand quite what it was he did; how the small fruits could swallow up so much of his attention. Yet her impatience evaporated once the fruits reached the kitchen, and the mere sight of a knife ruptured their tender skins into puddles of pink juice and pips.

The first Coronavirus lockdown started a month after my grandad's wake, throwing my grandma and thousands of recently bereaved others into the deep end of widowhood. Though we'd speak frequently on the phone, she became increasingly hard to get hold of as the months wore on and the afternoons grew light and warm. We were baffled as to what an 89-year-old could be doing in isolation that would keep her from picking up – and it wasn't until we were finally able to visit her that we learnt the reason, when she took us on a grand tour of her garden, which was, as usual, an explosion of colour and scent.

After poring over the petunias and admiring the azaleas, we reached the greenhouse, where a sharp tug and the harsh scraping of the so-called sliding doors revealed a fug of flowering tomato plants. The sight and the verdant, vegetal scent were so vividly evocative of my grandad, it took my breath away. 'They take a lot of work. I understand why he spent hours down here now,' Grandma smiled, pinching out some greedy side roots with deft fingers. Having never lived on her own, we had feared those long months of isolation would compound Grandma's grief to breaking point; yet in the close warmth of the greenhouse, tending the tomatoe plants that were once his, she'd felt connected to her husband on a physical as well as spiritual level.

We picked a few ripe ones and headed back to the house to eat them as he would have done: with cheese, on bread thick with butter. 'I think he'd be proud of me,' Grandma said.

Recipe: Grandad's 'Scallops'

Apparently, Grandad used to make these for my mum and aunt every Friday, and dish them up together with 'scraps' – the bits of batter leftover from the fryer. Even today if you went into a chippy and ordered scallops, you'd far more likely get these than the shellfish. Sadly the hassle and health risks of deep frying battered potato rounds meant they'd fallen from grace by the time Nicholas and I came along, though Grandma did make them for my brother and me after Grandad had passed so we could understand what they were, even if not quite what they meant.

Ingredients, for four
225g/8oz plain flour
1 tsp baking powder
Pinch of salt and pepper
220ml/8fl oz cold water
750g–1kg/about 1¾–2lb Maris Piper, Romano or
*   King Edward potatoes, peeled and cut into*
*   2–3mm/⅛in slices*
Oil, for frying
Tartare sauce, to serve

Method
First make the batter by sifting the flour, baking powder, salt and pepper into a bowl, then create a well in the centre and add the water. Whisk until smooth. Meanwhile, heat the oil in a deep fat fryer to 175–180°C and put the oven on low. If you you're frying

fish too, you'll want to make these in advance and keep them warm whilst you cook the fish.

Dip the potato slices into the batter, ensuring they are well coated.

Make sure the oil is at temperature before you put the potatoes in. Fry them in batches for about 4 or 5 minutes per batch, then drain on kitchen paper, sprinkle with salt and serve with tartare sauce.

12

Bread Ahead's Amaretti Biscuits

Meals to make money, and make colleagues friends

'You could basically devote a whole chapter to biscuits,' laughs friend and fellow food writer Gurdeep. Our conversation has moved to colleagues. Neither of us has colleagues anymore – we're both freelance – but we have between us spent 20 years observing workplace dynamics, and how food and drink play a part. We have both bonded over biscuits: the chocolate digestives or, better still, Hobnobs over which you can strike up a conversation with even your most tiresome colleague; the one with whom you share nothing but a preference for dark chocolate ones. 'You don't choose your colleagues any more than you choose your family, but food becomes a way of feeling empathy with a person,' Gurdeep continues. 'Even if you have nothing in common at all, you can probably bond over a tub of M&S flapjacks,' the very sight of which is enough to spark a shift in the office dynamic, as news of their presence ripples around the room.

The flapjacks say, relax. They say, let's lay down tools for a moment. 'Food serves several functions, one of which is to give rhythm to your day,' says Gurdeep. 'Breakfast, coffee, lunch, tea in the afternoon are the allotted pause points, which is why it's so exciting when something happens outside of that. It's the *unexpected* allowance of a pause.' Gurdeep is a musician, as well as a food writer. His depiction of meals as the metronome of the working day makes treats sound like a sax solo, breaking out and delighting the audience with its joyous deviation from standard mealtimes. 'The biscuits come out, or the flapjacks, or the birthday cake and people think, "Oooh, we don't normally break at 4 p.m.". It's a thrill,' he continues – because unlike everything else in the office, food and drink represent *not* working.

It reminds everyone in a tangible way that we are first and foremost human beings: that our need to eat eclipses our need to work; and that whilst we might disagree with colleagues on many things, we can all agree we like eating. Like mufti day at school, the appearance of baked goods in the office kitchen deprioritises the need to work. Once the lid is off the biscuit tin, it is license to graze, says Gurdeep. 'I think that's why it's such a bonding thing. You are coming together over an experience that isn't work and is generally removed of anything threatening.' Perhaps that is also why communal food in offices tends to toward the benign: chocolate biscuits, tubs of flapjacks, Krispy Kremes and Pret sandwiches, all of which come under the category of food which is agreeable, but devoid of character. In a room of strangers who may or may not become friends, it is helpful to have things which are simply universally pleasing.

Or at least, that is how it seems at first, when whoever has bought or baked the treats opens the tin or packet. 'Help yourselves guys!' comes the eagerly anticipated refrain – and everyone looks round at everyone else, not wanting to be the first to rise. Invariably, the greediest goes first and, once that seal's been broken, people start to drift over from their desks at varying speeds according to who they are and whether there's any advantage in rushing. A tub of homogenous flapjacks will prompt a slower drift than a selection box of Celebrations or Krispy Kremes, for example, where being slow may entail missing the Maltesers Teasers or Original Glazed.

It is at this point that people's personalities start to emerge, peeking through the sameness of the snacks like weeds through the paving stones. How quickly they move, what they choose – even how they eat it bel reveals ies the character that lives within their humdrum suit or uniform. 'Even when the food is the same, people find ways to express themselves, and colleagues observe it,' Gurdeep agrees. 'You notice that person who puts crisps in their Pret sandwiches, or doesn't eat the crusts, or only eats a certain filling or flavour.' Much is made of people's willingness (or not) to get a round in, yet I think it is the nuances of food and drink that are so revealing, and which are such fertile grounds for connection. We may still be in the office. We may even be at our desks. Yet in the moments we are eating or drinking, we are liminal creatures, somewhere between work and home. We are neither entirely employees, nor entirely ourselves.

Working for a publishing company based at Borough Market meant my former colleagues and I were spared more generic treats, favouring artisanal pastries and cakes from the market traders. Yet our quirks still came through in how we approached our various delicacies. My former colleague Viel was always first to the communal spread, and never worried about taking that final lonely biscuit – the one left out of excessive politeness. Mark was next, and earned himself the nickname 'secret snaffler' by nibbling throughout the afternoon, every time he got a glass of water from the sink. Ellie and I were always last and would opt for the smallest portion of everything except the almond croissant from Olivier's Bakery. Our collective favourite as an office was amaretti biscuits from Bread Ahead: fudgey, dense with ground almond, dusted with icing sugar and just the right balance of sweet.

These details feel meaningless now I no longer work with them, but at the time their discovery seemed to bring me one step closer to knowing my colleagues. As these observations accumulate – and with them, our ability to respond to them – so the potential to make friends with our co-workers increases. There is care in saving a plate of sandwiches for someone, but there's even more care in remembering that egg mayo is their favourite filling, or ordering their latte with oat milk not almond when you're getting a coffee round in. Once you know your colleague needs – like, NEEDS – her porridge and banana every morning between 8 and 9, you know that her missing that window is a warning sign she might be stressed. Likewise, if she's having homemade lentil soup for lunch for more than two days in a row, you know she's in her overdraft and won't want drinks after work. This is when you're approaching friendship. 'When you know your colleagues' routines so well that you notice when they are deviating from them – I think that is when you feel really close,' agrees Gurdeep. 'That's when you feel liked and cared for.'

Gurdeep remembers working in the food development department at Marks & Spencer, and forging a food bond with his colleagues that was premised as much on knowing each other's routines as it was breaking out of them together. 'I knew my assistant Emily always had porridge at her desk, did yoga at lunch, and that by 3 p.m. she needed sugar. Yet every so often she would have a croissant for breakfast, and I would say "Oh, you're not having porridge today" – just to check everything was okay,' he recalls. Mostly, it was. Mostly, Emily just fancied a croissant. Yet noticing someone's routine to the point where you note the deviation makes them feel loved, he continues, because it makes them feel seen and, in some small way, understood.

With about two thirds of our daily meals eaten at work – and that's without snacks or drinks – the opportunities to relate to colleagues through food are numerous. Working at places like M&S or Borough Market meant there was probably a greater emphasis on this than in some industries – yet you don't have to work in food to value making a cup of tea for your colleague and knowing as well if not better than their spouse how much milk they want. There is such intimacy to that knowledge, to being attuned to the rhythm of each other's day even to the point of falling in sync around certain meals or drinks: be that a mid-morning cuppa, afternoon beers or Friday morning bacon butties to soothe the night before.

Mark, Ellie, Viel and I all had our own routines in our office – yet alongside them there ran our communal routine, like planets orbiting the sun whilst rotating on their respective axis. Our first full office cuppa was at 8.30 a.m., and usually made by me. The second, for Mark and Ellie, was post lunch, whilst I held out for our third collective cup, made by Ellie at around 4 p.m. If it was a Friday, we'd have an extra cup mid-morning, to go with our weekly treat from Borough Market. This ritual was dubbed Friday Feeling, and was upheld even more religiously than afternoon beers.

I am not sure precisely when we introduced Friday Feeling to our office, but I do know this weekly treat proved formative in cementing the fast friendship that still exists between us. It started, as so many Friday rituals do, on Thursday afternoon with an animated conversation on what sort of sweet thing we all fancied. As Friday morning broke and I reached the market to pick our treat, it gathered pace. I'd send photos of available biscuits and cakes, generating a flurry of opinionated WhatsApps; then triumphantly bring the chosen one back for us to enjoy. There was fun to be had in dividing filled doughnuts into four even pieces and taking the piss out of whoever spurted vanilla crème down their shirt; and there was love to be shown in sacrificing the sliver of tart with the best ratio of filling to pastry to whoever was having a bad day.

Even bad baked goods were good, in that they united us in our revulsion. The gluten- and dairy-free banana muffin, devoid of structural integrity, moisture and seemingly bananas, remains an entertaining reference point to this day. Again, this isn't just foodies; both Mum and her friend Louisa recall occasions their colleagues brought 'unusual' food back from holiday, only to discover these alleged delicacies didn't quite translate to the office. If my mum couldn't find anything she deemed delicious enough to take back to her team, she'd buy the thick chocolate biscuits from M&S, on the premise that it was the flavour as much as the thought that counted – and her team would prefer those to some Bulgarian boiled sweets.

'Some European sweets – and British sweets, like rock – are vile,' laughs Louisa, whose most successful holiday spoil of recent times was a pot of honey from Greece. 'The team are still raving about it a year later.' Louisa neither works in food nor even eats much of it, as previously mentioned; yet she absolutely understands its value to her company when it comes to building rapport. 'Food is such a bonding source of conversation,' she explains. The favourite game at their Christmas party is the tasting game, where she does a blind tasting between super-market own-brand foods and branded foods. 'We've done it with everything from digestives and jelly babies to baked beans and ketchup, and the team love it.' It prompts aminated debates and childhood memories. Every morning when her team come in, they ask each other what they had for dinner, and what they had with it. 'They are particularly keen on discussing the accompaniments; it's never just the mains,' she laughs. A few hours later, talk turns to lunch – at which point many will decide to club together on a takeaway.

The sharing element of food is vital, she's observed, whether it's holiday food, treat food or someone's Deliveroo spring rolls. Inspired by the success of the honey, Louisa recently brought a big tub of ManiLife peanut butter to the office. 'Everyone got a spoon and ate a spoonful straight from the tub,' she recalls. It was hardly hygienic – but therein lies the significance of sharing. Illogical as it sounds (and indeed is), sharing germs is one of the hallmarks of intimacy. Having a bite, having a sip, trying a bit of someone else's food is one of the distinguishing features of a loving relationship. On a basic level it demonstrates trust – I am trusting that Ellie isn't knowingly diseased when I take a spoonful of her ice cream, and vice versa – but more than that, it suggests a shared appetite for greater familiarity. As knowing and caring about each other's food rituals is the line between colleagues and mates, so dipping into the same shared tub, Tupperware or bowl is the Rubicon between mates and close friends.

Of course, you don't have to go so far as sharing germs to build team solidarity – but it does help if you eat together, as those in many European countries have long been conscious of. The idea of eating 'al desko' is beyond the comprehension of anyone I've spoken to from Scandinavia, France or Spain. Even the concept of a sandwich was met with genuine shock by people in San Sebastian when my cousin and I visited. 'To have a sandwich here? It is like NO: when we are eating, we are sitting down with people and enjoying our produce,' declared our host Maite, outraged.

There, even the most mundane meetings demanded some *pintxos*, just as in most Swedish companies it is mandatory for all employees to sit down and have *fika* (which roughly translates as coffee, cake and chats). In Denmark, the concept of *fællesskab*, which is loosely the feeling of trust and togetherness, is inextricable with eating together; something that applies as much in the workplace as it does elsewhere. Then of course, there is France, where the long business lunch is practically enshrined in their national identity. That the practice of going for lunch collectively as an office is, in Britain, largely confined to the work Christmas party is sad – but it is also a missed opportunity.

A few years ago I started doing some work for the cheese retailer Neal's Yard Dairy, and was struck by how big and well equipped their the kitchen is in their head office in Bermondsey. I commented on it to one of the directors, who told me that every day team members take turns to cook lunch, then sit down and feast together at the long, wooden table occupying the centre of the room. It was vital to how they worked, he said: on a practical level, by boosting communication between different departments; but on a personal level too, by ensuring each employee feels valued and can foster meaningful friendships. As a result Neal's Yard Dairy has always felt more like a community than a company – even to outsiders like myself, who never partook of the company lunch but has always been treated to meetings over cheese.

It is difficult to measure the impact the pandemic-fuelled rise in working from home has had on our professional relationships, to know just how much closer to colleagues we'd be now if we'd continued to drink and eat with them. Much was written during the course of Covid about the absence of 'water cooler chat', a catch-all term for conversation that happens in the office and over food and drink. In these liminal spaces around the kettle, Krispy Kremes or indeed the literal water cooler, small talk can lead to bigger discussions which researchers have identified can result in colleagues helping each other to destress, or work through a problem. Mug by mug, Original Glazed by Original Glazed, biscuit by biscuit they build and cement friendships between colleagues – which leads to better staff retention long term. Indeed, so significant was water cooler conversation deemed, some companies even tried to replicate it remotely using hastily invented apps called things like Water Cooler and Donut; yet they were largely unsuccessful.

Such spontaneous moments of connection in areas of transition are, by definition, almost impossible to design.

It was Covid that forced the closure of our tiny publishing company at Borough Market, forcing Mark, Viel and I into freelancing full-time and Ellie into an editorial position at a local council. There, most people come into the office one day a week since various lockdowns were lifted. She enjoys it, but misses the intimacy forged by making each other tea, sharing food and knowing everyone's culinary quirks. Of course, the ritual of talking about food can continue over Zoom – but talking about bread is not the same as breaking it together: knowing who wants cheese, who wants ham and who wants their mayonnaise on the side.

Some employers identified this distinction early on in the lockdowns, and were swift to instate Zoom-based drinks, coffees or lunches. In what seemed to me like a clear testimony to the value of eating the *same* food, new companies sprang up to deliver wine tasting kits, healthy lunches and sweet treats around the country so colleagues and associates could experience it together whilst apart. A friend of mine works in shipping, one of the last bastions of the long lunches in Britain. Not to be defeated by something so parochial as a global pandemic, they sent out huge hampers, brimful of pâté, caviar, cheese and wine to themselves and their clients, in order that they could recreate their very important long, boozy business lunches online.

That is the other side to food at work, observes Gurdeep: food as powerplay. 'Food has a power dynamic at work that it doesn't have elsewhere in your life. If you are trying to strike a great deal or win new business over lunch, that is a very different dynamic to getting a load of Pret sandwiches in for the team.' The latter is collective, designed to provide a common ground for connection and morale; the former is more of a negotiating tool, with potential for division as well as union. From choosing the wine to paying the bill, through navigating a possibly unfamiliar menu, each mouthful has the potential to reveal the nuances of the relationship between the two diners, and to direct it. A restaurant-owner friend recently created a bidding war between five different publishers for a book from a relatively unknown author, simply by taking them all out for a fancy dinner and sending them home with the manuscript afterwards. He wasn't an agent; if he had been, he'd have known the days of wining and dining prospective publishers are almost over. Yet the author was a friend of his and talented, and more than anything else my friend knew the power of good wine and good food.

He knew that, ultimately, those who are well fed will always be more amenable toward the feeder. He knew that the conversations are richer, the tangents more explorative, the criticisms more constructive and the compliments more fulsome in the presence of a decent meal. Though commonly derided and rarely welcomed, the business lunch or dinner works a magic that cannot be replicated without food and drink. It is more contrived than the water cooler chat, in that both its occurrence and purpose are planned in advance; but the course of conversation is inevitably shaped by the courses served. No matter the intention or action of the diners, the arrival of the bread, the presentation of the wine, the perusing of the menu all have the potential to create common ground or break and dispel any existing tension. The conversational thread sparked by some perfect chips could lead to a sensational deal, or it could simply end in dessert.

I no longer have colleagues, but I have made many friends as a freelancer, for of course nowhere does food and drink feature in working relationships quite so much as in the food and drink industry. Despite fierce competition for staff, coverage and customers, the chefs, producers, PRs and journalists who fight for them are exceptionally close knit. There are fast friendships between the owners of competing PR firms, between independent butchers, bakers and cheese retailers (most of whom are former employees of Neal's Yard Dairy). You could argue this is just correlation; or that the sort of people the food and drink industry attract tend to be a sociable sort who readily form friendships. Yet it's hard to believe the near-constant presence of food and drink doesn't play a significant part.

When every meeting involves eating, or at least talking about eating, the uniting, pacifying and diverting joy of food is never far away. Food is our work – but it is life, first and foremost. Remembering and rejoicing in that is our job, and what makes our relationships thrive. In a working culture where food and drink are considered mere support acts for serious business matters, we forget the role they play in forging the connections that make business happen; whether that's whispered gossip by the water cooler, or loud declarations of support brought forth by oysters, roast partridge and three bottles of vin de Bourgogne.

Recipe: Bread Ahead's Amaretti Biscuits

Few incentives to get out of bed are quite so powerful as the prospect of plucking these warm off the stall at Borough Market in the morning. Ambient, they are beautiful: soft, with just the lightest crunch to their icing-sugar-dusted exterior. Warm, they're like a freshly baked heavenly cloud which an angel has swooped down and offered you a morsel of. For Matthew Jones to share this recipe with me is therefore nothing short of miraculous – and I am eternally grateful to him and his book *Baking School: The Bread Ahead Cookbook*, in which it appears.

Ingredients, makes 18 biscuits
2 egg whites
188g caster sugar
300g ground almonds
1½ tsp honey
1 tsp almond extract (please don't use one that's been sitting at the back of the cupboard for the last 10 years)
100g icing sugar, for dusting

Method
Preheat the oven to 180°C/160°C fan/gas 4, and line a couple of 45cm x 38cm baking trays with baking paper. Place the egg whites in a bowl and whisk until frothy, then add the caster sugar and whisk until soft peaks are formed. This will take a good few minutes. Add the rest of the ingredients, apart from the icing sugar, and mix with a spatula until incorporated.

Cut the dough into 18 pieces, each weighing about 30g, then roll them into balls. Spread the icing sugar in a tray. Put the balls of dough into the tray, roll them around, then leave them to sit for 10 minutes, to absorb some of the icing sugar. Now carpet-bomb the balls with icing sugar, really packing it on. Carefully place the sugared amaretti on the prepared baking trays, leaving a little space between them because they will puff out a bit.

Bake for 16 minutes, until golden brown, then take them out and leave them to cool a little. Perfect with an espresso (or a cup of tea, if you're part of our office).

13

Diana Henry's Linguine All'amalfitana
Feeding solo

'Wait, hang on. Back up. You're saying that you, who writes about food, talks about food, and loves food more than almost anyone I know are missing out on one of the greatest culinary joys out there?' My friend Rosie looks at me in genuine astonishment across an antipasti platter, an olive half-raised to her mouth in a dramatic pause.

We're talking about eating alone. More specifically, we're talking about solo dining, which my dining companions for the evening, Rosie and Lizzie, love and which I go out of my way to avoid. 'I just – spending time with people I love is one of the best parts of eating out for me,' I counter. 'Without them there, I don't really see the point.' Where's the pleasure in a tantalising menu if you can't discuss it with your companions, I continue, gesturing to the menus which, sure enough, we'd spent the last five minutes deliberating over. How can you make the most out of a good wine list if you're drinking by yourself,

I ask, raising the glass of chilled white I'd just poured from our bottle of Trebbiano d'Abbruzo.

Indeed, how can you justify drinking at all? Drinking for me was about companionship: relaxing over the first glass, catching up over the second and letting loose by the third. You can't have that sat by yourself at the bar. 'Drinking alone' – the very words paint a sad and lonely picture of someone drowning their sorrows, presumably because they have no friends. Nor did eating alone seem much better: being unable to share olives or tear the last slice of sourdough in two, being confined to just one starter, having no one to compare notes with or swap mouthfuls of main course and no shared memory to call upon after the meal has ended. Sure, we might not depend on our tribe to hunt and cook like our ancestors. We're no longer inclined to liken lone diners to lions and wolves, like Epicurus once did. But to argue, as Rosie and Lizzie both were, that dining alone was a positive experience – well, that was an evolutionary step that I was mentally incapable of.

This is not to say I am blind to the joys of eating by myself, period. Though for a long time being alone come dinner invariably translated as not having dinner at all, ten years of reading and writing about food has persuaded me that in the right circumstances, *feeding* oneself can be a source of comfort – even joy. The verb matters. Where eating alone suggests some passivity, feeding is active: you are hungry, you choose your food, and you cook it for yourself, just how you like it. Where eating alone feels like something that could have been forced upon you, feeding yourself feels like a conscious choice.

Writing her fifth book in the wake of a traumatic divorce, Bee Wilson found she felt pleased when she cooked for herself

– even when those meals took almost no effort. In fact, simple bowl foods like salad, soup and minestrone were particularly appealing. 'It would have been a different thing if I was alone all the time – if I didn't have the kids most of the week. Maybe I would have felt lonely. Maybe my disorders would have resurfaced. But there sometimes is a way in which feeding yourself – holding your bowl in both hands, feeling cosseted by it – can take you back to a more simple relationship with food' she says, cupping her hands around her mug of coffee to illustrate her meaning.

Somehow the bowl is significant: the feel of it, the smells that emanate, and the permission it gives to eat wherever *feels* right, be that the table, bed or sofa. Where a plate spells company – or at least formality – a bowl is inherently intimate. A bowl implies it is your food, time and, crucially, your space, whereas a plate suggests you might like to share. Whatever the contents, the tall edges and smooth roundness of a bowl feel both more personal, and better able to protect you from the chaos of the world around you. Holding a bowl of Diana Henry's anchovy pasta which I have made myself with extra Pecorino and garlic, I feel the rare and warm sense of completeness that comes from understanding and looking after yourself.

'It's like going back to yourself,' Diana observes, when I ask her about her relationship with cooking and eating alone. 'You go through the routines – peeling, chopping, slicing – and you're paying attention, but you are also absorbed. When I am cooking something I love, I feel I am coming back to my core,' – so much so that when she experienced neuropathy in her hands, as a result of an autoimmune disease, it was not being able to handle a knife that distressed her most. She recalls trying to slice the soft flesh of raw scallops upon returning from hospital and being unable to get her knife through them such was the loss of feeling. The effects were short-lived, thank goodness, but for a few days Diana was paralysed by the thought of losing something fundamental not just to her professional life, but to her very being; her core.

Of course, cooking and eating define Diana and Bee far more than most people; they're food writers. Nevertheless, they are right that even when it's made by you, for you, food has the potential for connection and love. The mistake I and so many others have made is to regard food made for oneself as mere fuel. 'Why bother?' is the familiar refrain echoed by those facing the prospect of preparing a meal for one. Why not just have toast for dinner? Why bother with breakfast? Why take the time and trouble to pour milk onto muesli in the morning when you can have a muesli bar on the way to the station, casting an idle glance at the back of the packet to check the contents as you swallow the last dry mouthful before boarding the train?

'Why bother?' Grandma said in the weeks and months after we buried my grandad. Overnight, their early morning tea-and-ginger-biscuit ritual fell by the wayside. By the time the first lockdown hit, a mere month or so after his death, their Sunday night supper of 'something on toast' had become her usual main meal. With no one to cook for, she simply didn't cook at all – so that as the rest of the country embarked on making sourdough and banana bread, she reverted to rolls and shop-bought cakes (she still treated herself to a small afternoon tea each day, to our relief). 'It's cooking for and eating with others, that's where the pleasure is for me,' she replied when we tried to cajole her into cooking over the phone.

The meditative pleasures of cooking described by Diana and Bee were lost on my grandma, who for 70 years had cooked out of duty toward her husband, hotel, children and grandchildren. That's not to say she didn't enjoy it, but that the enjoyment always lay in her love for those she cooked for, rather than cooking itself. Whilst I – eventually – came to see cooking as a way of satisfying my mind as well as my body, my grandma cooked for the end result: to nourish her family and guests, and to receive (then bat away) the ensuing compliments. Whilst I lingered over Nigel Slater's descriptions of 'languidly bubbling' cauliflower cheese and pumpkin cooked until 'fragrant, tender, on the verge of collapse', my grandma glanced at recipes (if she was even using them; she rarely did), pursed her lips at the flowery language and cracked on.

None of this is surprising. We are products of very different generations. Where I have lived my whole adult life with the option of skipping meals, ordering in or just eating cereal, my grandma has never had a choice. From the day she married my grandad to the day he died 71 years later, she cooked for and ate with him three times a day, every day. It seems ridiculous to imagine this 92-year-old woman coming to regard cooking as self-care; as a means of reconnecting to herself.

For me the joys of cooking are largely contemplative: engaging my senses, reading new recipes or cherishing the repetition of one I can cook with my eyes closed. To turn to the burnt and spattered cookbook page outlining Diana Henry's linguine all'amalfitana – anchovy pasta, for short – is to return to a familiar friend. I no longer need the recipe, but over the years certain lines have acquired a talismanic quality: counting eight silvery-brown anchovies out of jar, peeling them apart like

Velcro and chopping them roughly. Cutting a hunk of Pecorino off to munch whilst I grate the rest into a snowy mound. Each memorised step serves to reassure me, right down to the final drizzle of olive oil she recommends finishing with. Linguine all'amalfitana is a recipe I cook on good days but, like all good friends, it is there for me on bad days also. There are days when I cook it in quiet, personal celebration of an achievement. There are days when cooking it is an achievement in itself.

Once upon a time, recipes made me feel lonely. I'd pore over the *The Guardian's Feast* supplement or leaf longingly through the latest Ottolenghi book, lusting after the stuffed aubergines with coconut then dismissing it because I couldn't justify such extravagance myself. My conversion was a gradual one. It began with Diana Henry's *Simple* – source of my beloved linguine all'amalfitana – and grew from there to Rosie Birkett and Nigel Slater via the ingredients I was daily surrounded by, working at Borough Market. *Tender: A Cook and His Vegetable Patch*, Slater's hefty first volume of vegetable recipes, proved particularly formative. Even the title spoke of a solitude more physically and mentally nourishing than anything I had ever allowed myself. Tender were the peas, broad beans and papery courgette flowers blossoming in Nigel's garden, but tender too was this gentle cook who shelled, podded or stuffed with goat's curd, and wrote about it: creating dishes which lightened my heart and fed my stomach, even if I felt alone.

Tender is not a 'single person's cookbook' – perish the thought, frankly, though I know some who swear by them – but the recipes are reliable, and demand little in the way of skill or ingredients. All Nigel asks is that you appreciate your produce – 'the beauty of a single lettuce, its inner leaves tight and crisp' or the 'rough feel of a runner bean between the fingers' – and that you engage with their transformation into creamy soups, pert salads and light scones.

'Bake until soft and squishy,' dictates one instruction, for baked finger aubergines, yoghurt and cucumber – one of the first dishes I made from this book. Nigel appeals to all senses, in the most seductive way possible, and he writes in a way that's peculiarly personal – the upshot, perhaps, of his famously solitary disposition. In his recipes, as in his life, the pleasures of eating start with the cooking; the instructions and the anticipated enjoyment are entwined together within every sentence. The pleasures are in cooking and eating, he teaches – not in serving the needs of others, or merely meeting your own needs as efficiently as you can.

Again, what matters is that cooking like this feels like an active choice – to feed myself, rather than eat alone. To nourish myself because I'm able to. It's a feeling that's hard to access if money's tight or aloneness has been forced on you; if you've been widowed, locked down alone thanks to, say, a pandemic, or are going through an unwelcome. To this end I am wary of romanticising cooking as the best means of forging a healthy, loving relationship with food and yourself – because today's prevailing narratives of food as self-care, cooking as therapy and 'cheeky' takeaways don't cater for everybody. My grandma will readily batch-bake 12 lemon drizzles for a cake sale at my aunt's school, but she'd sooner fly to the moon than bake Nigella's Mine-All-Mine Sweet and Salty Chocolate Cookie for One.

One of the magazines I write for regularly is called *delicious*. Like all food magazines, it has the usual spread of feasts, cakes and family dishes – but it is unusual in regularly including articles and recipes that will appeal to and work for one person. Its editor is Karen Barnes: a kind, bright and considered woman, and one of the first editors to commission me when I started freelancing. I once asked Karen why *delicious.* did this when most food media didn't bother and she told me they get a lot of emails from readers who are newly on their own, thanking them or seeking support.

'The pandemic highlighted the need to acknowledge those who eat alone; for them to find joy in our pages, as well as recipes that meet their requirements,' she told me. Many of these emails thank her team for providing columns and features about food which aren't recipes at all; which are just there to inspire, or provide comfort or joy. She cited one heart-rending email from a man in his 80s, whose wife had recently died, and who had never really cooked before. His wife had always cooked from *delicious.* he told Karen, so he wanted to continue the subscription to feel connected to her.

That this man might find solace – companionship, even, within the magazine's pages is testimony to the potential media has to 'rekindle one's enjoyment in food, especially if you are of a certain age and your life has been constructed around feeding others or being fed by them,' observed Karen. 'It is so important those people feel acknowledged; that putting food on the table feels important, even when you are the only one there.' If reading *delicious.* magazine helps someone eating alone feel better connected with themselves, others, or memories of others then that's a victory in her eyes – whether they're cooking from scratch or peeling the lid off another microwaveable meal.

It is difficult to underestimate the significance of being able to bond over food even when we're apart, and how interwoven that now is in our eating experiences. Where once 'sharing a meal' entailed sitting down at the same physical table, these days to 'share' food is as likely to mean posting your sourdough on social media or reading the same guide to making a starter as it is physically breaking bread with someone else. When I lament to Kaori the anthropologist the missed bonding opportunities that come with us eating alone more, she begs to disagree. 'People share food all the time. Just because it's not face to face doesn't mean there's no intimacy,' she counters. 'Sending pictures on email or WhatsApp, posting to social media – it's still a way to get to know people.' Factor in the multiple conversations generated by food documentaries, cookery shows and restaurant reviews and you have a whole ecosystem of connections rooted in sharing food. 'You can't taste it,' Kaori smiles, 'but it's there.'

I might not be able to convince my grandma to cook for herself; I will never convince her that cooking is self-care. But I can and do talk to her about food often: the food she grew up with, the food she cooked for us, and the food I cook for myself. I ring her for her advice on scaling quantities – something she excels at, thanks to hotel catering – and my mum and brother call her for advice on baking and pastry. She reads every single article I write, even the most fatuously 'foodie', so that she can inhabit the world I live and work in. My grandma doesn't need to cook for herself to feel connected through food, I've realised. She is connected through the conversations, advice and memories we share.

Besides, with time it has become apparent that my grandma rather relishes the freedom to not cook, and to eat when and what she wants to. Those shop-bought cakes? She genuinely likes them. It might seem mad to those of us raised in an era when ready-made cakes are so cheap, but when she was young, they were the height of decadence. That she can now both afford and justify an apple pie from Mr Kipling is a small illicit pleasure which satisfies her and no one else. Indeed, to have someone else there would probably detract from her enjoyment of a cake that she loves but would never dream of serving to others – something which reflects a broader shift in attitudes toward people who live (and by extension, eat) by themselves.

'There're a lot more people living on their own, or on their own within a shared house, and that has brought a lot more emphasis on the person rather than group,' observes Kaori. 'It's okay now to be an individual in your own space, having what you want when you want. There's no practical reason to make meals social; on the contrary, it can be limiting, eating with somebody in a way that goes against what you would normally do yourself.' Left to my own devices, I'm constantly reheating my food. I might microwave my meal two or three times during the course of eating it. This enables me to keep my food at the temperature I most like, which is piping hot, whilst eating at the speed I most like, which is painfully slow. I eat everything from a bowl, including beans on toast and jacket potatoes, and with the exception of beans on toast and jacket potatoes, I like everything with frozen peas. I have a ruminant's appetite for vegetables, which I will cook huge, sharing-size portions of – safe in the knowledge I won't need to share.

In company, I tend to keep this on the downlow. I eat a reasonably sized portion of vegetables at a reasonable speed and confine my peas to pea-appropriate dishes. Even in front of housemates, I have tried to prevent these eccentricities from appearing too extreme. To be able to indulge in them fully; to add peas to my linguine all'amalfitana and burn my mouth with my third reheating because I've taken two hours to eat one meal, feels like a communion with myself and my idiosyncrasies. For someone who is extremely extroverted; who comes alive in the company of others, cooking and eating alone reminds me of who I am when it's just me.

So why was I so immune to the joys of doing this within the context of a restaurant or bar? I could understand why Rosie and Lizzie were baffled. I pleaded extroversion, but this argument didn't wash with Rosie, who is herself a classic extrovert. On the contrary, that is partly why she loves it, she tells me. 'I get so much juice from the company of others that having dinner *with* someone is always an event beyond the food. I love it so much and it's my favourite activity with friends, but sometimes I like to give myself the thrill of having my own company. It removes the negotiating over an order and makes me decide exactly what I want. It's a mindful practice: at the absolute most I'll read a book or a zine, but I'll generally just sit there and let the pace of the meal dictate my thoughts. I've had some of my best ideas while sat completely by myself, waiting for a main.'

Where I imagine myself getting out my phone to assure myself and others I have friends, Rosie never gets her phone out during a solo meal. In fact, she dismisses my fear that I'd be judged by my fellow diners out of hand. 'I think there's a self-imposed stigma around solo eating,' she says. 'No one actually gives a shit if they see someone dining by themselves. If anything, people look at a solo diner and think, I wish that were me.'

Not that dining solo is the sole preserve of the contented and confident. Nor is it necessarily unsociable – quite the opposite, say Rosie and Lizzie. Indeed, the very restaurant in which we are dining as we chat – Mora in Leytonstone – is where Lizzie headed by herself when she was dumped by an ex-boyfriend. In need of red wine, pasta and space to process her thoughts in a space that wasn't her sofa, she sought out her local Italian and its familiar, solicitous staff. 'When I was grieving, I broke down over some cornichons in Sodo in Clapton, and the waiter looked after me so kindly,' Rosie rejoins. Were they simply passers-by, this would feel like sympathy. Yet with the simple, soulful addition of good food and drink, such kindness felt like love.

I am fascinated by those who eat out alone. When I wrote about it a few years back, I was struck by the number of people who had made friends for the night or even a lifetime with staff and fellow diners. Chefs described people teaming up to share small plates so they can sample more of the menu. When they start sharing, they start talking; some even end up on spontaneous dates or nights out. Rosie once found herself in a lock-in with a restaurant's owners until six in the morning, having struck a chord with the barman. It's a great way to meet people – I'm told – or just to observe people and enjoy the warm convivial, hubbub of the restaurant. Yet more than anything else, I'm told time and time again that dining alone is an act of self-love.

'If I need to eat, why don't I do it with the same kindness and generosity to myself that I would show anyone else?' observes my local publican, Nick, who eats out at every opportunity his job affords him. Indeed, the words 'love', 'kindness' and 'generosity' – from the restaurant staff and toward oneself – crop up again and again. Through his psychotherapy course, Stefan at Olivier's bakery has been 'slowly discovering that the philosophy of honouring oneself is an essential element in any therapeutic endeavour – not in the form of narcissistic aggrandisement, but in terms of taking the time to honour our relationship to the self,' he told me, when I interviewed him for one of these articles about eating alone. 'Any added romance we may enjoy . . . is ultimately born out of the effort we put into our relationship to ourselves.'

I would love, for the sake of the narrative of both this book and my own life, to tell you I have since taken myself for dinner and enjoyed it. I haven't. I tried it once for the sake of an article and thought the experience was bearable, though would have been bettered by friends. I do, however, now go for a cocktail or glass of wine, in places which feel a little bit fancy. I read my book or do some work – I'm too self-conscious to simply sit there – and I lend half an ear to well-heeled people discussing their affairs.

I've been surprised by how therapeutic I've found it – and that's not just 175ml Viognier talking. When you consider the gestures from other people that make you feel loved, they are often the unnecessary ones: the hugs, cards and phone calls you didn't even know you needed until they were there. Sitting in The Cavendish in Marylebone and savouring the taste of wine I can't afford alongside expensive olives I'm glad I'm not sharing, I've found the same is true of the things I do for myself: be that a glass of wine out, or a bowl of pasta and peas on the sofa. Circumstances matter. I agree with Bee that were solitude forced upon me, then it would be more destructive than nurturing – but where I have chosen it, it feels like an investment; one which helps me better connect with myself.

About a year after one of my articles about eating alone was published, I had the chance to catch up with Stefan during a quiet moment at the market. He'd been meaning to thank me, he said, because since the article featuring his interview came out, he'd started dating one of his regular customers. Apparently she had always been quietly soft on him, but it was through this article that she discovered he was single, giving her the courage to ask him out for dinner. Rereading Stefan's quotes, I am stuck by his prescience regarding his relationship to himself through food, and how it would inform any meaningful relationship he might have in the future.

I am struck by the way the now-couple connected over bread without breaking it, through an article about eating alone which one read and the other contributed to. By being themselves, by themselves, and being content with that, they found each other and could share their bread, as it were. I may never eat out alone; but sat on my sofa with my linguine all'amalfitana, WhatsApping my friends about Stefan and ordering some liquorice online for my grandma, it is quite clear that people can connect over food without necessarily eating together – and that those connections are enriched by our first feeding ourselves.

Recipe: Diana Henry's Linguine All'amalfitana

It's almost embarrassing how much I love this recipe; how often I've turned to it in times of heartache, happiness, half-marathon preparation, ennui or exhaustion. Being premised on store cupboard ingredients (and peas, if you're me) it is cheap, easy and incredibly quick to rustle together. It's like my teddy bear, which sits on top of my headboard on good days, and inside my bed on bad; it's simply there for me whatever the mood, whenever it calls.

For this recipe, and the permission to print it, I am incredibly grateful to Diana and her book *Simple*.

Ingredients, for two
165g linguine
3 tbsp extra virgin olive oil
2 cloves garlic, crushed
½ tsp dried chilli flakes
50g walnuts, roughly chopped
8 really good-quality cured anchovies, roughly chopped
½ tbsp flat-leaf parsley, finely chopped (optional)
Grated Pecorino, to serve

Method
Cook the linguine in salted boiling water. Meanwhile, heat the olive oil in a sauté pan (or shallow casserole dish) and gently fry the garlic, chilli flakes and nuts for a few minutes. Don't let the garlic brown.

Add the anchovies and press them in the pan with the back of a wooden spoon. They'll melt in the heat.

Before the pasta is quite ready, add three-quarters of a mug of the cooking water to the pan, then drain the pasta and add that to the pan too. Finish cooking the pasta in the sauté pan until it is al dente. The cooking water will reduce to form a sauce with the other ingredients.

Add the parsley (if using) and season. You can add another slug of extra virgin olive oil if you want to. Serve with grated Pecorino.

If you're adding peas, add those to the pasta water when you've about a minute of cooking to go and drain with the pasta.

14

Reconsidering the Oyster

Fare for the heart

If only my own experience of romance had been as seamless as Stefan's. Though no stranger to the old saying about the path to true love, I didn't expect mine to be quite so cobbled, nor to contain so many forks – both literal and metaphorical – in the road. A love life that began inauspiciously in Pizza Express Pinner has since woven itself into a tapestry of anecdotes and life lessons. Not all feature food; one involves an abandoned reservoir underneath Finsbury Park, where a guy took me to his friend's illegal rave on a first date. Not realising much of the candlelit reservoir was still filled with deep, stagnant water, I took a step in the wrong direction and fell in. Another came of my breaking my ankle on the way to a date, and soldiering on regardless. Yet another was born of my trying to win back someone I regretted dumping by sending him an eraser with 'For big mistakes' written on it. 'Do you think,' my friends ventured gently, when I wondered why he hadn't come running back, 'he might have got the wrong idea?'

Most of them, however, are food and drink related – not just because that's what most dates involve, but because beyond conversation meals are the main medium through which we express ourselves and how we feel about others. A meal is a shared experience, whether it's a takeaway pizza or a tasting menu, and for prospective couples this dance of culinary courtship – the 'Here, try some of this,' 'Can I try yours?', 'You have the last piece' charade – can be as revealing as any verbal or physical exchange. Even the choice of drink sets the tone for the evening. My friend Lizzie once went on a first date to a pub, ordered a glass of wine whilst she waited for his arrival – then he turned up and ordered hot chocolate with whipped cream and marshmallows. It was 7p.m. It wasn't the not drinking she minded, it was the fact that meeting in a pub had been his suggestion and, as well as making her feel uncomfortable, the mismatch between their drinks seemed to point toward incompatibilities beyond his hot chocolate and her large Chardonnay.

'It's a form of signalling. Food signals who we are culturally, and it makes us who we are physically – which makes eating together a form of real intimacy,' observes anthropologist Kaori. In fact, many societies parallel it with sex, she says, because it is something which makes you one together. 'This means eating and drinking together can make you one at the outset – but it can also go in the opposite direction.' Unlike other potentially dividing lines – politics, sports, etc. – eating and drinking is a secular sacrament. 'What you put in your mouth literally becomes part of you, which makes the idea of someone eating something you dislike or disapprove of difficult to shrug off.'

I am reminded of the time I found myself on a date with a journalist who revealed he reviewed weaponry for *Janes Defence Weekly*. 'What, giving grenades a score out of ten?' I joked. 'Yeah, a bit like that,' he responded. The worst disclosure was not his job, however, but when he told me he had eaten dog, horse and whale, and 'wouldn't say no to cat, out of curiosity', as if he thought I'd be impressed by his ability to eat both endangered animals and household pets.

Few things can give you ick quite so quickly as food does – and few things are so immediately indicative of someone's character. In hindsight I should have known that the man who took pocket chopsticks to the pub to eat crisps with would be particular in other areas of life, and that the man who was repulsed by the idea of sharing food would struggle with intimacy. 'It's not just you,' he'd say as I looked longingly after plates of golden, guacamole-crowned nachos and bowls of salt-crusted chips. 'The idea of sharing with anyone repulses me.'

The guy who took me to a party in the underground reservoir on a first date eventually embraced veganism, together with the rest of his counter-cultural friendship group. The man who drank Huel meal replacement powder because he was 'too busy to chew' struggled to make time for me. By way of contrast, the man who rocked up to a date by the Thames with a paper bag of pink radishes and pat of butter to share was as delightfully odd and genuine as his appreciation for something so small and honest as a fresh radish suggested.

By the time I was 30, I had developed my condiment theory: the idea that what a person added to their food could provide some clues as to compatibility. Looking back on some of my worst romantic choices, it seemed the warnings were written in the sauces: kisses thick with garlic mayo, scorching obsessions with chilli, the guy who feigned a preference for savoury flavours then proceeded to slather everything in sweet chilli jam and worst of all, the guy who couldn't resist squeezing the jelly-ish mustard you get in yellow bottles in insalubrious pubs directly onto his spoon.

Yet for much of my teens and early 20s the concept of culinary compatibility eluded me, in part because I didn't eat, but mostly because – with the exception of Pizza Express – you don't really have dinner dates at that age. At university the height of food-based affection consists of gifting someone your hottest, cheesiest chip on the way home and stealing your housemate's milk to make tea the next day. The only significant food romance moment I remember at Durham was a date in Treats café, where I resisted the temptation to order my usual gingerbread latte because my date – a Robert Lowell-loving fellow English student with a copy of the *TLS* under his arm – had ordered a very serious sounding black Americano.

This was the guy I'd go on to send the misleadingly labelled eraser to. We dated twice: first in Durham, then again in London in our early 20s, when dating largely meant pubs, parks and – at best – squeezing into Gordon's near Embankment station for a cheap bottle of white. There was one notable exception: when I went round for dinner and was proudly presented with gravadlax he had spent three days curing. The half side of salmon occupied most of the fridge in his shared flat, wedged between cheap lager, outdated milk and a nearly empty jar of pesto sporting a furry white coat of mould. That he had put so much money and care into a casual Tuesday meal spoke of his feelings better than any words could have – and when I came to regret parting ways, it was that gravadlax I kept returning to: blushing with beetroot, fragrant with dill and invested with time.

It takes time to prepare a meal with love. It takes some money, of course, but time is by far the more telling ingredient. It doesn't need to be hours; it could be as labour intensive as dumplings or as simple as pasta, but without time, money feels cheap; it is what rich people use to compensate for the time they haven't spent with loved ones. I have never felt so unloved as when an ex-boyfriend said he'd 'treat me' to breakfast, scrambled eggs with smoked salmon, then wolfed it down and left the house before I'd sat down, as 'punishment' for my seeing a friend he didn't like. By way of contrast, the first occasion Ukrainian food writer Olia Hercules went round to her now-husband Joe's house for dinner, she was blown away by the lengths he had gone to impress her with ordinary ingredients treated with extraordinary care and time.

'I thought it was funny that he wanted to cook for me; I didn't know he could cook. Then I came round, and it was next level,' she remembers. I'm at their house in East London for a cuppa, which is taking a while because I've told Joe I like it strong and milky and he's a stickler for getting food and drink right. 'He did a whole roasted cauliflower and, knowing I was Ukrainian, made a dill oil from scratch – which must have taken ages,' she continues. When she first met Joe, Olia was a single mum and stressed with trying to work and parent. 'I neglected myself for a while. I could go all day without eating,' she says. Within a year of their seeing each other, she had put on a much-needed ten kilos. 'He makes breakfast and lunch for us, and we stop and sit down together. He makes sure I look after myself. For me that's been a big thing about food and love.'

Joe is vegetarian. Olia is not and, being the writer of mainly Eastern European recipes, still sometimes cooks meat and fish for her and their two children. That this is not and has never been a source of tension is testament to the strength of their relationship, and their willingness to compromise. If Olia is cooking with meat she will make a vegetarian version for Joe, who respects and supports her wanting to eat meat. When she turns to him halfway through our chat and declares she would like more roast chicken in her life, he smiles and agrees. On date nights, they share a hot, molten Vacherin Mont d'Or. 'It's the first meal we had after our son Wilfred was born, and it was magic,' Olia says, her eyes shining. 'Now if it's the two of us having a date night, that is what we'll have, with wine, boiled potatoes and gherkins.'

Vacherin Mont d'Or is one of the main reasons I could not date a vegan. Reasonable compromise is all very well, but I draw the line at not being able to share a vat of melted cheese on a winter's evening. Even if, as Olia and Joe prove, you don't have to be aligned on all your culinary principles, there needs to be harmony in how much you enjoy food. There can be harmony in you both not enjoying food, of course; in eating Shreddies for dinner, and looking elsewhere for the joy that sustains your relationship. In the case of couples I know for whom food equals fuel, their relationship works because they feel and eat the same way. Yet whilst my partner might not revel in spring's first soft, citrusy goat's cheese or winter's ruddy forced rhubarb with quite the same zeal as I do, I need them to not be immune to their pleasures. 'When food is such a fundamental part of who you are, it's difficult to connect to people who don't get it,' says Diana Henry, who once had a disastrous relationship with a man who wasn't that fussed by food. 'Why wouldn't you look for that joy every day?'

A friend of mine once dated someone who, if he particularly liked a dish, would assemble the perfect forkful so that she could experience what he was experiencing. It was such a touching example of sharing one's vision of the world – like taking someone you love to the top of a favourite hill or building and telling them to stand... just... there to get the best view. Were that person to turn around and ask what they're supposed to be looking at, you would feel a deep disconnect in your respective perspectives. It's not always necessary, but sometimes it's vital the person you love sees the world through your eyes, Diana continues – unlike her ex, who saw eating as 'an obstacle that just got in the way'.

At worst, mealtimes are just like this: sites of tension, battle-grounds or silent retreats broken by the bleak scrape of cutlery. At best, though, the shared experience of eating and drinking together weaves a sensory thread throughout your lives. All of my most enduring partnerships have had a particular food or drink as a leitmotif: frozen yoghurt, gin, squid, beetroot ravioli, anchovy toast – mouthfuls which capture moments we felt particularly at peace or in sync with each other. Sometimes that's on account of the food or drink itself; often, it's born of an experience or feeling that food has, by some strange transmutation, come to stand for.

For Viv and her husband Jon, that food is pineapple pizza; specifically, Hawaiian pizza from Papa John's which they order so regularly Papa texts Jon with a discount code each Friday.

Such is the strength of their signature dish, I knew of it long before I learnt where it came from – yet its origin story is not what I or indeed anyone else would have thought. When I ask about it, they tell me Hawaiian pizza was born of a bout of food poisoning that had struck them both down whilst hosting Thanksgiving years ago. Only by the following evening were they ready for something to eat. 'We were watching *Big Mouth*, and a character said, "I could murder a Hawaiian". We turned to each other and said, that is exactly what we want and need: Hawaiian pizza. So we ordered this enormous pizza and we were so depleted, it felt like manna from heaven. Now we order it whenever we feel like a boost. It's our comfort food.'

That this – for Italians – blasphemous pizza could become 'their' meal is the last thing you'd expect from Viv and Jon: a cultured, well-travelled couple renowned for their brilliant dinner parties. Yet the bonding experience out of which their regular Papa John's was forged was about far more than the pizza itself. It's all very well fetishising the food you eat together, Viv says – but there is ultimately a flipside to that process, which is 'the other end', she says, delicately. 'It sounds gross, but they are intimately connected. And you cannot avoid that, if you're a couple. You can't pretend otherwise if you're in it for the long haul.'

Being thrown together to ride out food poisoning in a single loo is not pleasant – but it is formative, Jon argues. What the Hawaiian captures is not so much the romance as the resilience of Jon and Viv's love, even when life isn't great; even when, as Jon puts it, 'there's no dignity left and nothing to hide'. Their penchant for cheap pineapple pizza points toward a broader truth about food's potential to root a couple in the reality of who they are – or, alternatively, to create a false premise for their being together. I have found this countless times when I have pretended to like or dislike something in an effort to project the version of myself that I think my date wants.

I've chosen natural wine to prove I'm a foodie; suffered Pizza Hut to prove I'm not; faked a taste for foie gras, fruit cake, fermented cabbage and dozens of oysters. In short, I have not always been 'real'; and even before that lack of realness was evident in the relationship, it was evident in what we ate and drank. Of course, there are few things more real than sharing a pizza after 24 hours of sharing a toilet. Yet you don't have to go as far as that to find couples connecting authentically over meals, in ways which are all the more romantic for appearing not to be. Angela, for example, shares a love of plane food with her husband, John.

'We get excited when the trolley comes. Then we go through our trays and say to each other "Crackers – nice! Cheese – nice!" whilst people are there with their bags of Pret and Wagamama's,' Angela chuckles. 'I don't know why. We could make that food at home. I think it's the togetherness of it,' she muses: the careful peeling back of the foil lid; the joint exclamations at the contents; and their ability to laugh at themselves as their bemused fellow passengers look on.

I can't help but wonder about the time they discovered they both liked plane food. Had one mocked the other for their enthusiasm or feigned an indifference toward the fridge-cold rolls and tinned fruit salad, this endearing culinary ritual might never have materialised. Had they not been completely themselves, they might never have established this symbol of togetherness which has endured throughout their relationship

– to the loving amusement of their children, Sophie and James. 'They despair of us. I despair of us! I say to John "Come on, we need to look cool about this",' Angela smiles, 'but then the trolley comes and we just can't help ourselves.'

Fake commonalities are not the same. I know this, having faked so many oysters. The pop and tinkling pour of champagne, the crowning with lemon and tabasco, the loosening of the glistening mollusc from its shell – it is beautiful, but it is only a bonding experience if both parties are genuinely enjoying it; otherwise, it's just an endurance test. On past dates I have washed any proffered oysters down with large, hasty gulps of champagne, in an attempt to disguise their taste, and my facial expression. More recently however, I decided to share my ambivalence toward these bivalves – partly because I felt comfortable doing so, mostly because this date – my now boyfriend, Chris – was a genuine oyster-phile, and I knew I wouldn't be able to fake my appreciation.

I thought the revelation would put an end to my braving oysters; in fact, I found myself more determined than ever to like them. With time, my persistence has become a source of amusement for both of us – particularly the resigned face I pull each time I'm presented with one – but it was born of my wanting to share in something Chris loves, and loves to share. That early honesty has paved the way for a ritual that feels 'real'; which reflects both of us as individuals, and as a couple with a similar humour and similar views on sharing at mealtimes. I can't pretend I enjoy the oysters themselves; but I do genuinely enjoy the process of anointing them with lemon, cheersing with their shells, knocking them back together and then assessing whether *that* oyster could be the oyster that has finally won me round.

'The idea of flirting through food is universal and historical,' says Kaori. Literature is littered with it. Film is full of it. It's basically a musical genre. 'You find out what your intended likes, and you court them over dinner. You get to know someone, and establish their preferences, and through that establish if you are compatible. Eating is a pleasure, and it is a special, intimate thing to eat something you both enjoy.' The dance of 'Do you like this?', 'How do you like that?' – it's like seduction at one remove, she continues. After all, the only activity that is as multi-sensory and intimate as eating together is sleeping together – which could, incidentally, be why most first dates revolve around coffee or wine rather than dinner. If you can be open about your food preferences – and ideally establish some similarities – then that should bode well for other areas. 'If someone only likes Subway and isn't willing to try anything else, they probably aren't going to be there for the long haul.'

Certain foods and drinks, therefore, are entirely non-negotiable. For me, they're cheese, seafood, tea, wine, fruit, bread and pasta. The man I dated who didn't like hot drinks was a non-starter: there is too much love to be found in that first drink of the morning; in taking it in turns to rise, stretch, pad to the kitchen and brew a cuppa in the right mug to the right strength with the right ratio of milk. Every morning my friend Emma needs strong coffee in a pale-yellow mug, and every morning her husband Rob makes it for her, in the mug he meticulously washes up every evening. So demonstrative is this gesture of the depth of Rob's affection, Emma's dad referenced it in his speech at their wedding, noting what it said about his attention to detail and daily consistency.

In short, food is rarely just food – at least not where relationships are concerned. It is a litmus test, a memory, a means of communication and a measure of values. 'One thing which is nice for us as a couple is how aligned we are about spending money on pleasurable things like eating out, or getting a delivery,' says Jon. For a while Jon and Viv worried about just how aligned they are when it comes to Deliveroo – 'As in, it really only takes one of us to float the idea and we're doing it,' Jon laughs, 'but then it gives us both pleasure. Paying for that doesn't make either of us anxious or put out.' Their flexibility, their openness to new experiences and their love of bringing people together – all come through in Jon and Viv's attitudes to meals. One of the characteristics Jon loves in Viv is how thoughtful and inclusive she is toward others – a trait which is beautifully evidenced in the spreadsheet she has detailing the dietary requirements of their friends and family. 'No one ever has a separate meal. They are always included. People always feel they will be looked after and their needs will be catered for, whether they are vegan or vegetarian or allergic to nuts. It's such an indication of how Viv is as a person,' says Jon, 'how she is always bringing people in.'

To watch Jon and Viv throw a party is to watch a couple completely in sync, who know their respective strengths and have honed them such that to be hosted by them is to be briefly immersed in the warm current of their dynamic. As Viv shouts hello from their galley kitchen, where she'll be putting the final touches to dinner, Jon will greet their guests and pour drinks. Once dinner is done, Jon will pick up the plates and pick up where Viv left off in the kitchen: clearing, wiping, washing and drying whilst she relaxes and enjoys that precious hour when the eating has ceased and the conversation and the wine continue to flow.

There's a rhythm to the way Jon and Viv entertain that is both fun and unflustered – encapsulating perfectly who they are as a partnership. 'I like cooking, but really value the point where I know my job is done, and I can hand over to Jon,' says Viv. Similarly, Jon enjoys focusing on the cleaning, preferably with his headphones in and a podcast on. Neither wants the other in their space whilst they crack on with their respective roles. 'I like doing the dishes. I like to have a job. I don't want us both cooking, or both doing the washing up because society dictates that's more equitable,' says Jon. Fridge magnet wisdom has it that couples who cook together, stay together, but Viv disagrees. 'Enforced couple time is pointless unless it is something you both enjoy.'

Mealtimes are a ritual through which love is cemented and expressed – but that doesn't necessarily entail you slaving over the same hot stove together. On the contrary, most couples I know say what matters most is their eating together, and each having a part to play in achieving that goal. Even Olia and Joe, who work in food and are highly accomplished cooks, balk at the idea of cooking together. 'We are very different cooks,' Olia says of her and Joe. 'I am neat, and Joe is messy.' 'I am not messy!' Joe retorts. 'I just like to harness the energy of the world.' Either way, when it comes to the kitchen, they are better off charting their own course literally and metaphorically.

'We'll do different dishes. Olia might do bread and pickles, whilst I might do something outside with fire, for example,' says Joe. It's been a journey, but we are now very comfortable in how we work.' Having roles creates structure and a rhythm for meals which cooks and diners alike find reassuringly familiar – necessary, even. Neither my dad nor my stepfather cook much, but they are meticulous about washing and clearing up, to the point where they bothfind it irritating if my mum or stepmum try to help.

That these roles are often gendered goes without saying, yet there are plenty of examples to the contrary in both heterosexual relationships and same-sex ones. The most important thing, it seems to me now, is agency: feeling you're playing your part out of love for your partner, and choice. When a past boyfriend designated me sous chef, it was not because I wanted to be, but because he liked being in a position of power. By way of contrast, when Angela brings out a battered copy of an ancient Jewish cookbook called *The Way to a Man's Heart*, I am startled – but Angela has subsumed this text and made its outdated narrative her own.

'John can and would cook, but he prefers I do it, and I do it because it pleases me,' she says. 'It sounds old fashioned, I know, but I like nurturing my children and I like nurturing my husband. When you do the same thing day in day out, you are reinforcing the bonds between you, and so long as there's respect there – and there is – I'm happy we have defined roles.'

Angela likes *The Way to a Man's Heart* because it's full of 'homely food – food that feeds and brings people together'. Such food is timeless, even if the title has not aged well. It is her only cookbook, which she's had for 30 years – longer, as this is her second copy, bought when she lost the first in a house move. Its soups, casseroles, rissoles and cakes have appeared throughout her life with John and with their children. They are their staples: the meals they have eaten together almost every day.

Only now do I realise the aptness of this word 'staple' for those foods which bind us to those who eat them as regularly as we do. For me, meals are the fulcrum; the steady, sumptuous beat to which our days, weeks, months and years play out. They are the punctuation marks to life's chaotic sentences: shit can and will happen between meals, but eventually you will have to eat. To understand the value of that precious first cup of tea in the morning; of the 'Fuck it, let's have Papa John's' pizza on Friday night; of the pure happiness brought by plump, perfect ravioli bursting with beetroot is to understand the value not just of meals, but of all that meals can signify: simple pleasures, time spent together, the change in seasons, human ingenuity, discovery and familiarity.

My friends and family remember my more ridiculous dates by naming them: Cthulhu for reservoir man; Chopsticks for the one who ate crisps with them; Bosun Bird's Eye for the man who bragged about his homemade fish fingers; James VII because I dated two Jameses and my Scottish father insisted on the Scottish title. Those men who have mattered, I remember by shared menus. I recall our first dinner out, the first dinner I cooked – invariably something from Diana Henry – and first brunches, blinking at each other in the bright light of the new morning. I remember drinks that brought us together, and drinks we broke up over, putting the bars in question out of bounds for years.

Over the course of a decade of dating here, London's restaurants and pubs are pockmarked with memories only I can see. It is a city of forked roads both smooth and cobbled. It is an increasingly foodie world, in which I've walked, dined, laughed, literally and metaphorically lost myself, and learned so much about what love is – and isn't – when it comes to food. The risk of finishing this book with a chapter about romance is that it suggests romantic love is *the* love; the love to which all others lead, which finally completes the picture. In reality of course, it is just one piece, which makes no sense without the rest of the jigsaw puzzle and the image on the top of the box, too.

Which means this isn't an ending. Food and love take many forms, and those forms are constantly shifting – even sometimes diminishing as we change and mature. That's part of their joy: the potential for there to always be new tastes to discover and people to befriend, as well as familiar faces and foods to fall further in love with. Meals are sometimes the means, sometimes the medium, and always the thread that runs through us and binds us. Over half-empty wine glasses and second helpings of crumble, mugs of morning tea and toast with scrambled eggs, Mr Whippy's slurped on a park bench, food and love come together and work in tandem: the befriending, falling and feasting mirroring each other in a multisensory metaphor.

After nearly ten years, Mum's friend Louisa has finally stopped dieting; she enjoys tea and cake with my mum – their joint favourite meal – and her husband no longer dines alone with the dog, Teddy. My mum, stepmum, dad and stepdad have built such a good relationship, they now meet regularly for dinner without the kids there. My grandma, now 93, has found a whole new set of friends to have coffee with and bake for.

As for me: for once, for now, my hungry heart feels full.

Recipe: A work in progress

EPILOGUE

Shortly after submitting the manuscript of *Hungry Heart*, Chris decided to work out how many hours his mum had spent making his favourite dish, chicken rice. Though neither of us can remember why, I suspect this was prompted by yet another chat about food, relationships and the connection between them. The revelation of this connection had become my lens on the world; like a favourite radio station, or those sunglasses you love so much you wear them at the first sign of spring.

Though made up of just its titular parts, chicken rice is deceptively time-consuming: the chicken stock is homemade, the rice cooked within it, and the chicken – also cooked in stock – must be perfectly poached and smooth. The dish is served with finely sliced cucumber, soupy stock and two different homemade sauces: ginger, and a dark soy sauce enriched with chilli. The answer? 830.4 hours, or five weeks without sleep over the course of Chris's 35 years.

They say you can't measure love, but if you could I imagine it looking a little like 830.4 hours spent making your son's favourite dinner. The same will be true of family meals around the world, of course, it's just rare that one stops to make the calculation. Chicken rice is particularly laborious, but even simple meals add up with repetition over time. This number is the most explicit example I have seen of food and love's connection – but there have been many others, all demonstrating food's power to sustain present relationships and forge new ones. My hope is that, by sharing a few of these examples, I might inspire readers to keep the story going by finding or forging their own relationships through food.

I wrote most of this book in Quo Vadis, a restaurant and members' club in Soho whose charismatic head chef Jeremy Lee is the embodiment of *Hungry Heart*'s concept. Every day Lee makes a point of walking through the lounge and dining room, greeting everyone with 'Darling!', an air-blown kiss and a quick chat if there's time. Last December, during an inevitable talk of Christmas and our respective traditions, Lee told me he and his siblings still made exactly the same Christmas dinner they'd grown up with, right down to his granny's spiced marmalade sponge. 'My parents made the marmalade together. They spent all day shredding peel,' he smiles. 'They loved to cook, and the rest of the year it could be French, Scottish, Italian – but come Christmas Day it was full blown traditional. There was never any question of change.'

Now Lee's parents are no longer around, it feels all the more important to conjure up their presence around the table come Christmas. They are with them in spirit but they are also with them in the food: in the roast goose, Eliza Acton mincemeat and that spiced marmalade sponge. Food and memory are deeply entwined, as we've learnt, and food at Christmas has a particularly mnemonic quality. The yearly basting, stirring and feasting serves as a multisensory portal to Christmases which have gone before, and the people who were with us then, which is why we cling to certain dishes with a borderline religious zeal.

Of course, Christmas dinner can evolve, too – and those evolutions can be equally emblematic. My paternal granny's grapefruit and dried apricot salad is the Christmas breakfast at both my parents' houses, my mum having fallen in love with it when my parents were together. Mum's Christmas Day is a mishmash of loves, in fact: her ex-mother-in-law's grapefruit salad, her mother's Christmas pud, my dad's kumquats and my stepdad's bottomless appetite for turkey sandwiches, which means getting a bird three times bigger than necessary. Every Christmas dinner tells a story, but seen through the lens of love certain nuances can emerge that may previously have been overlooked.

'They fell in love in the kitchen, and I'm the result,' my friend James says poetically of his parents, who first met in a shared house upon moving to London from Malaysia and Singapore. They went on to make their home in west London, running restaurants and weaving their culinary heritages together – a weaving that is wonderfully expressed in their Christmas Eve meal. 'We like the European tradition of having seafood on Christmas Eve, but we always have an Asian dish,' James explains. 'A recent tradition is ginger lobster noodles, and oysters served with fresh chilli and garlic sauce instead of Tabasco.' Similarly, acclaimed pie maker Nokx Majozi recently told me her mum always made their traditional dessert, malva pudding, when she was growing up in South Africa – but her

London-born daughter wanted it to be more Christmassy.
Now they incorporate mincemeat and serve it with custard.
'We make it together,' she says. 'It's her Christmas, plus my
heritage. It's beautiful.'

Festive food is fertile ground for stories of food and love
– your own, and other people's, which is why the question of
Christmas dinner dominates conversations come December.
Being offered a small insight into how and what others eat
at Christmas is like an Advent window into other worlds. In
the run up to a recent Christmas, Lizzie's aunt Bunny invited
me carol singing, followed by drinks and nibbles. No sooner
had her husband, Thomas, learnt that I wrote about food
than I found myself downstairs in their cellar-turned-pantry:
admiring his array of homemade jams and pickles proudly
displayed in gleaming Kilner jars along wooden shelves.

The 'tour' concluded with Thomas' more squat creations,
hidden from sight under greaseproof paper: his membrillo. He
made it every year, he explained, and had done for decades but as
word of its joys spread, he was forced to ration it. 'It takes a long
time,' he said – a long time, and a lot of quinces, which he collects
from gardens around their south-east London home. Now only
a select few are beneficiaries of Thomas' quince cheese so you
can imagine my joy when he carefully peeled off two pieces,
wrapped them, and handed them to me like presents. 'Don't
tell anyone,' he warned, ushering me upstairs and I thrilled at
having a small, secret morsel of this revered festive delight.

Of course, not every Christmas anecdote has been so
wholesome; yet even in those cases, food has often been the
redeeming feature. My friend Ben broke up with his first serious
boyfriend in a sandwich shop a week before Christmas – a

surprisingly good time to do so, he notes, it being the season for feasting, family and friends. Twelve hours after the break-up chat, having been passed from friend to concerned friend like a parcel, his appetite returned at the McDonald's near Bank station in London. 'I hadn't been to McDonald's in years – but my friend and I had walked and talked for hours,' he recalls. 'He had toothache, so needed something soft, and I was in emotional turmoil.' Two inaptly named Happy Meals later, and Ben says something in their relationship shifted. 'We still talk about that day as being significant in our becoming closer friends.'

One tries not to break-up over food – especially not in a restaurant. Yet it happens, and more often than you might expect it does. Conversation falls apart, the centre cannot hold, and before you know it, you're sobbing into your pumpkin velouté and sourdough roll. Waiters and bartenders I know say they take looking after unravelling couples as seriously as they do those tying the knot – more so, for the recently engaged need neither nourishment nor distraction. Years ago, my friend Kit broke up in the Italian restaurant Pulpo and can still recall the kindness of the staff who waited on them: topping up their drinks as the couple tearfully dismantled the remains of their relationship, and quietly clearing the remains of their meal.

The care and attention we receive at the hands of hospitality is a love that's often overlooked – though in its own way, it can be just as powerful. The most compelling example I've experienced was when Mum and I finished our long cycle through France, on 8 September 2022. We'd been in the saddle for two weeks straight, and were eagerly looking forward to greeting my stepdad, who had driven down to the finish line to greet us. Yet as Mum and I freewheeled triumphantly into Biarritz and my stepdad's waiting arms, news broke of the late Queen's being ill in Balmoral; and for the rest of the day, instead of celebrating, we scrolled anxiously through the social media feeds and the news. Eventually we resolved to enjoy our time: the Queen would live, because she always did, and she'd be the first person to disprove our not having a drink in this historic city. So we found a wine bar in the waning sun, put our phones away and ordered some olives. Moments later, the maître d' came over, bearing a solemn expression and four glasses of crémant.

'To your queen,' he explained, setting three softly fizzing glasses down and raising his glass respectfully. 'I'm sorry for your loss. She was a great lady.' So it was that we learnt of Queen Elizabeth II's death not via Twitter or the BBC, but via a kind French restauranteur and some free crémant. It could not have been more apt, nor more moving; and we thanked him through tears as we raised our glasses; struck by the love he'd shown both us and our queen through a gesture that both marked and made this moment unforgettable.

The pages which follow are blank, not because I've no more to say – I could and perhaps one day will write a second volume – but because my biggest hope for this book is that it will inspire you to tell your stories. These could be significant recipes, menus or memories of meals out or in. They could be how long your mum has spent making chicken soup, or how much money she spent on Petit Filous when you were young. They might focus on food you've shared with family, friends and colleagues, or on meals you've savoured solo. They could mean love, or its bedfellows, loss and longing. I thought I had finished this story of food and love but so long as we've the potential for eating, drinking and loving each other, it has the potential to go on.

Food stories

Meal maths
No, not calories: the amount of time you have spent making your favourite food, or your loved one has spent making it for you. It's pretty straightforward – you just need to work out how long it takes to make, then how often you have it each week, month or year.

Festive feeling

What does your Christmas dinner look like now? What dishes have you added or lost over the years, and how does that reflect the people you've spent Christmases with?

Heartbreak hors d'oeuvre

What did you eat or drink during or after a recent break-up, and why? What did that meal mean to you, and who did you share it with?

Hospitable heart

What have been your most memorable meals out, and who have you shared them with? Do you have particular restaurants you go to with particular people? What role does service play in the importance of that place? Can you remember occasions when staff have been particularly empathetic, generous or kind?

Feeding solo

What is the meal you most enjoy eating by yourself, and why is it more enjoyable on your own than in company? Have you a socially unacceptable way of eating or combination of foods?

Food of love

Forget champagne, oysters, chocolate-covered strawberries and other clichés; what food says romantic love to you, specifically?

Sibling suppers

What meals remind you of growing up with your brothers and/or sisters? What were your shared loves, and mutual dislikes come dinner time? What games did you play with, during or over food?

School dinners
What were the highs, what were the lows, and how instrumental were these meals in fostering friendships?

Food and loss

What food or drink keep the memory of someone special alive?

Food and the future

What meals and mouthfuls could shape and deepen your relationships with family, friends or partner going forward?

ACKNOWLEDGEMENTS

When it comes to thanking those who made this book possible, it seems only right that I start with those who made me possible. My first and biggest thank yous, therefore, must go to my parents and grandparents, who fed me even when I didn't make it easy, and to my brothers Nicholas, Alexander and Angus for showing understanding and love far beyond their years.

Melanie and David, the word step-parent falls pitifully short of all you have been to and done for me; ditto the word cousin, for my cousins Joseph and Emily. Honourable familial mentions should also go to my aunts Deborah, Katharine and Wendy who, through the first few rocky years of my parents' divorce, did their best to provide stability for Nicholas and me; and to my great – 102 years old, no less – Uncle Gordon, who introduced us to gooseberries.

On a more practical note, this book wouldn't exist without my agent, David Luxton, and Ned Palmer, who introduced me to David after a long, wine-fuelled chat about cheese and writing. Thank you for showing faith in me and my idea and pursuing it relentlessly despite a pandemic and my periodic crises of confidence – and thank you to the Aurum team at Quarto for commissioning it, in September 2020. At times it seemed Richard Green, Phoebe Bath and Melissa Smith knew what I wanted *Hungry Heart* to say better than I did; thank you all for directing me so sensitively.

Of course, a writer is only ever as good as their editor, and in my years in journalism I've been lucky enough to work with some of the best in the business. A lifetime is not enough to thank my very first editor Mark Riddaway, for taking a punt on a small and desperately insecure 21-year-old and introducing her – via Borough Market – to the joys of food writing. I have worked with and learned from Mark every month ever since and am honoured to feel in some way his protégée. Mark my words, I owe you.

Many thanks must also go to subsequent significant editors: Jon Hawkins and Mike Gibson from Foodism, Olivia Walmsley from *The Telegraph*/*The i Paper*, Bob Granleese and Phil Daoust at *The Guardian*, David Ellis at the *Evening Standard* and Karen Barnes from *delicious.* magazine – all of whom have been generous and instructive in their commissioning and editing of my words.

Hungry Heart would be very slim indeed without the anecdotes, insight and recipes of all the people in it: Johnny Grey, Polly Russell, Bee Wilson, Kaori O'Connor, Diana Henry, Sandra Wilson, Emma Hawley, Claudia Fox, Jayshree Patel, Ravneet Gill, Gurdeep Loyal, Bex Lindsay, Viv Egan, Jon Gracey, Louisa Farino, Anastasia Miari, Stevie Martin, Lisa and Simon,

Lauren Bravo, Olivier Favrel, Stefan, Mesi of Mesi's Kitchen, Shuk Ng, Belinda Skipper, Emma Skipper, Ana Rose Sharkey, Jay Foreman, Daisy Buchanan, Charles Burch, Lizzie Burch, Rosie Beaumont-Thomas, Angela Corcut, Joe Woodhouse, Olia Hercules, Ben Salter, James Arumainayagam, Nokx Majozi, Max Kelen, Thomas Kelen and Jeremy Lee: thank you for sharing your stories and dishes with me. You have widened my lens on what food and love can be and enabled this book to appeal to a plethora of people, not just people who know me.

It will not have escaped readers' notice that several of my interviewees are friends, or friends of friends, or have indeed become friends by virtue of my speaking to them about *Hungry Heart*. It's hard not to become friends, when food and love is your subject matter, and nothing proves *Hungry Heart*'s conceit quite so well as the friendships I've forged as a result of it.

Nevertheless, my mother's wisdom rings in my ears: 'Make new friends and keep the old. One is silver, the other gold', and it is those olden, golden friends I am most indebted to. My family have always fed me, lovingly, routinely, occasionally desperately – but it is my friends who really taught me how to eat.

So thank you, Sophie. Your sunny, deeply thoughtful nature has guided, propelled and often carried me over the past 25 years. I don't know where I'd be without you, but it wouldn't be happy, healthy and writing. Lizzie, your warm heart and cracking good humour have either kept my sanity, or alerted me to incipient insanity. Both of you make me my very best self and only my very best self could have written this book.

A thousand thanks a piece to Skipper and Sharkey, who were with me when I wrote the proposal to *Hungry Heart* in Portugal. You have supported me as steadfastly in this as you have in so many other parts of my life and I completely indebted to your love, wisdom and patience. More thousands of thanks to my wife Ellie R, work wife Ellie C, Hatty, Emma M, Pippa, Lauren B, Rachel, Orlando Gilli, the Fat Buddhas and my former housemates Katie and Laura: you have laughed with me in good times and laughed or lifted me out of sad times and your joy, advice and kindness ripple through these pages.

A universe of thanks must also go to The Moonwalkers, who heard the idea for this book before anyone else, and who have played a starring role in both in encouraging me to write it and within its pages. Viv, Jon, Bex, Matt and Dougal – thank you.

Last in order of appearance (though not importance), thank you Chris, who came into my life halfway through my writing the book and successfully – if inadvertently – altered the course of both narratives. Thanks to your mum, Sue, for summing up *Hungry Heart*'s entire premise with one dish, chicken rice; and thank you for transforming its ending into a perfect beginning.

Index